42 Rules for Superior Field Service

The Keys to Profitable Field Service and Customer Loyalty

By Rosemary Coates
and Jim Reily
Foreword by Joe Pinto, Cisco

ſUPERſtaR press

E-mail: info@superstarpress.com
20660 Stevens Creek Blvd., Suite 210
Cupertino, CA 95014

D1082565

Published by Super Star Press™, a THiNKaha® imprint
20660 Stevens Creek Blvd., Suite 210, Cupertino, CA 95014
http://42rules.com

First Printing: May 2013
Paperback ISBN: 978-1-60773-070-5 (1-60773-070-7)
eBook ISBN: 978-1-60773-071-2 (1-60773-071-5)
Place of Publication: Silicon Valley, California, USA
Library of Congress Number: 2013936818

Trademarks

Warning and Disclaimer

Dedication

Rosemary Coates: For all my consulting clients who have taught me what is so important about field service and for my loved ones, thank you for always putting up with me.

Jim Reily: For all of my many mentors whose patience and guidance helped me learn life's important lessons and especially for my family who is a constant source of inspiration and love.

Acknowledgments

We are delighted that these executives agreed to be interviewed for this book:

- Morris Cohen, Wharton School, University of Pennsylvania
- Jim Miller, Google
- Dillard Myers, Cisco Systems Inc.
- Christine Parlett, Siemens
- Joe Pinto, Cisco Systems Inc.
- Damon Schingeck, Markem-Imaje
- Michel Yasso, MSR Consulting Group

Biographies of these people are available in the Appendix.

In addition, several other executives were interviewed but chose not to be listed by name. Some of the most valuable information came from these people. We appreciate the executives who took time out of their busy schedules to share their field service experiences and insights with us. We are very grateful.

We, Jim and Rosemary, also became great friends during this process. We did not know each other before the writing process began. But over the past two years, we have worked closely to finish this book. We appreciate each other's knowledge, skills, and hard work.

And last, but certainly not least, we are very grateful for Mitchell Levy, our publisher, and Laura Lowell, our executive editor, for believing in us and encouraging us along this journey. These are two very remarkable and talented people, and it is our privilege to know them and work with them.

Contents

Foreword by Joe Pinto, Cisco

Why do some companies thrive year after year, while their competitors fall by the wayside and either go out of business or are sold? The short answer is successful companies have loyal customers. These companies are able to acquire and keep good customers, who buy the company's products and serve as advocates with other potential customers. In a virtuous cycle, loyal customers provide consistently higher-margin revenues that successful companies use to field constantly improving products, provide outstanding service, reward employees, and generate excellent returns for their shareholders.

How do you turn a good customer into a loyal customer? Of course, you must market great products and solutions. But it takes much, much more. No matter how great your product and/or solution is, there will be instances where it does not perform adequately in the field. How your company reacts to those situations will determine, in large part, whether your customer becomes or remains loyal. Your ability to deliver superior field service, to quickly and effectively fix any issues that arise, will result in high customer satisfaction and lead to increased customer loyalty.

So how do you deliver superior field service? First step is to **read this book**. Rosemary and Jim have written a concise, easy-to-understand primer on service, which hits all of the key areas necessary to delight customers with your field support and make them loyal to your company. Both are well-respected executives with a wealth of experience in service and supply chain. They tell it like it is providing key operational insights and often breaking from the conventional wisdom to give you advice from the field that is battle tested; it works. In the end, it is all about how your customer perceives **your** commitment to their success. When they have business-impacting issues with your company's products and/or solutions, do you delight or disappoint them with your response? Delight translates to loyalty, disappointment to desertion. Read and follow the 42 rules and you will be rewarded with delighted, loyal customers.

Joe Pinto,
Senior Vice President, Technical Services
Cisco Systems Inc.

Introduction

We have a passion for field service.

Between the two of us, we have over 60 years of field service and supply chain experience, and that's a lot! We've seen military organizations, companies, and clients where field service is done well and others where field service is a complete disaster. And that is the reason we have written this book: to pass on the best practices and to help you avoid the pitfalls.

Before we started writing, we researched the available literature on field service, and there wasn't much in the way of guide books. So we embarked on this journey to inform people about how to run a field service organization that performs well and makes a profit. We believe field service is a key to customer satisfaction and loyalty in most industries. You need to be smart about it and informed regarding the components of field service.

In addition, the world keeps getting smaller. With the rise of the Internet, common global travel, global calling, texting, and ERP systems, businesses are free to order anything, anytime, and any place. Expectations are that customer service organizations are available 24/7 and that someone, somewhere in the world, will pick up the phone if you call for service and perhaps even respond within a few hours in any country. These developments have increased the complexity of field service and have caused many of our clients to rethink their strategies. To stay competitive, a lot of rethinking may be necessary.

And finally, most companies now recognize that there are big margins to be made in services. While companies may be experiencing downward price pressure on products, field service still looms large as a high-potential area for major profitability and customer loyalty.

For these reasons, we have written this book. We sincerely hope you find it interesting and useful. We have thoroughly enjoyed writing it.

1

Rules Are Meant To Be Broken

There are no steadfast rules in field service.

As you will read in the following rules, there are fundamental precepts that we support and that should be followed for successful field service organization and business. But we are the first to acknowledge that field service is a bit like the Wild, Wild West. There are all kinds of things you can try to have a successful operation. We encourage you to experiment a little and think creatively about your own organization in order to achieve the best results. Be a bit of a cowboy, and venture out beyond the corral.

Take defining the "perfect customer," for example. In Rule 9, we describe how you can identify exactly the type of customer you want and then systematically go about creating your business to develop this type of customer. This is a reverse rule for how most companies would develop services, but it works, and we can prove it. Break the old rules, and think creatively!

In Rule 11, we recommend you prepare for horrible disasters because we all know they are going to happen, and field service is likely a "first responder" for your customers. We encourage you to be very creative in thinking about and practicing various responses. Break all the rules of traditional thinking to respond quickly and effectively.

In Rule 26, we claim that inventory turns are irrelevant. This may be heresy to your financial organization, but in reality, the margins on spares and repairs are so big, inventory turns may be unimportant. Inventory management is one of those corporate supply chain concepts that really should be thoroughly examined within the context of field service. This is another rule that should probably be broken in a field service organization because, here, it just doesn't make any sense.

In Rule 34, we recommend that you transform your field service people into salespeople. After all, they are the ones talking to the customer every day about your equipment. You'll have to help your sales management organization get over this rule. They probably won't like it because they are reluctant to give up ownership of the account. Work with sales on this one.

The best organizations we have seen are high-energy, creative groups where feedback is welcomed and fresh ideas are always considered. The talented managers running these organizations spark new ideas and enthusiastically embrace different approaches. They round up the posse; they break the traditional corporate rules; and, as a result, they:

- improve customer satisfaction,
- enhance customer loyalty,
- improve margins on the services part of the business,
- assist in the selling process and in closing more deals,
- listen to their field service people and readily accept suggestions,
- demonstrate good performance measures,
- are respected in their own organizations, and
- are typically high performers.

We want your organization to be wildly successful. So shake things up a bit, put on your white cowboy hat, and use our rules as a springboard for running your organization. And don't forget to break a few rules, too.

Part I
Sales and Marketing

Delivering superior field service requires deep knowledge of your customers' business, how your company's products support that business today, and how you can provide better support in the future. The rules in this section will help you turn product failures into opportunities, acquire critical information about customer needs, understand and thwart competitors, and expand your service horizon to add profitable revenue to your company and build customer loyalty.

Sales and Marketing Section Rules:

- Rule 2: Product Failures Are Opportunities to Delight Customers
- Rule 3: Ask and You Shall Receive
- Rule 4: Form Customer Advisory Boards to Build Loyalty
- Rule 5: Know the Competition to Avoid Surprises
- Rule 6: Win Against Competitors by Servicing Their Products or Not
- Rule 7: Meet Specific Industry and Customer Needs
- Rule 8: Field Service Is Critical To Your Brand
- Rule 9: Develop the Perfect Services for the Perfect Customer
- Rule 10: Field Service Is Not Just "Break/Fix"

2

Product Failures Are Opportunities to Delight Customers

You will build customer loyalty if service is responsive and effective.

No one wants a product to fail, but it happens. The way you deal with failure can create significant opportunity to enhance customer loyalty. But, if handled poorly, it gives your customers the excuse they need to buy from your competitors.

Your customer views product failure as an emergency, especially if it affects business operations. Take a dentist, for example. If his or her vacuum system stops working, the office must shut down until it's repaired. This is inconvenient for the dentist, the staff, and the patients. It also represents loss in business revenue until the system runs again. This kind of situation is high priority for field service organizations servicing dental offices.

In industrial settings, when a product fails, you may have to deal with irate customers who have spent lots of money with your company. This can be a golden opportunity to show customers that you support them with speed and efficiency.

"90% of what I deal with starts as a problem, but I don't look at it as a problem. I look at it as an opportunity to delight a customer," says Michel Yasso of MSR Consulting Group.

Customer service organizations offer the following steps when first contacted by a customer with a problem. Field service organizations should follow the same steps:

- Empathize with the customer; do not make excuses.
- Don't patronize or talk down to customers; this will only make the situation worse.

- Really listen to what the customer is telling you, take notes regarding the situation, and ask for clarification.
- Remain calm even if the customer is not.
- Apologize, if appropriate. Say something like, "I'm sorry you are frustrated; let's see how we can resolve this situation."
- Promise to try to fix the problem or to try to find a solution. This will ease the tension the customer has created. The customer is looking for a resolution. Then do what you promise.
- Answer confidently, and take responsibility for assisting, even if this means you must refer the case to someone else.
- Give the customer a time when you will get back in touch—one hour, four hours, one day, etc. Then be sure you call back at the appointed time. Keep following up at regular intervals until issues are resolved.
- Take action to get the customer operating as soon as possible, or obtain information and estimates when this will happen.
- Write clear, concise reviews of incidents. Document issues and resolutions. Keep notes about anything that may assist others who deal with the customer in the future.

Your customers know that things will break, but they will be upset anyway. Your ability to react quickly and efficiently is crucial.

Sometimes, field service doesn't go as expected. It may be appropriate to escalate to your customer's executive management, especially when situations involve significant disruption in business. In these cases, your service executive or director should call the customer C-level executive and apologize. Give realistic estimates for repair, and perhaps, tell the executive you are going to make suggestions, after the issue is resolved, about how to avoid future disruptions. This may include things like more frequent maintenance or the purchase of redundant systems for critical business processes.

Professor Morris Cohen of The Wharton School notes, "The objective of service is to generate customer satisfaction. And satisfaction results from the difference between the customer's perceptions of service versus the customer's expectation for service. If the perception is greater than the expectation, the customer will be satisfied or even delighted." The opposite is also true, no matter the objective quality of service. So, set realistic customer expectations, and strive to exceed those. You will have delighted, loyal customers.

3 Ask and You Shall Receive

Field service organizations should not to make assumptions about customers.

World-class field service organizations ask for feedback relentlessly. Marriott Corporation asks every guest every time if everything went well with their stay. On their web site, Marriott provides a place for written feedback that a guest might not want to deliver otherwise. They also provide a customer service feedback card that you can complete and mail back. These feedback collection methods help Marriott to continuously improve their service. The result? Marriott has the most loyal customers in the global hotel business by far.

We can certainly learn from Marriott's relentless quest for customer feedback, but in the field service business, this is not enough. We also need to gather feedback and intelligence from our own internal departments, partners, and competitors to understand our true market position and the potential for improvement.

First, we need to find out and thoroughly understand what field services and product support our customers want and need to be completely satisfied and loyal to our brand. This is not merely a review of what we are capable of delivering but a "blank sheet" approach to what the customers actually want from our products and services. What we have been offering may not be what customers are looking for. Use a series of questions around the following categories as they relate to your customer's business:

- What can our products and services do to improve your business?

- What is your expected response time when you have a product performance issue?
- What do our competitor services provide that you would like to see us provide?
- What is your expectation for telephone or e-mail communications when problems arise?
- How do you rate our field service personnel on competence, professionalism, and courtesy?
- What does it take for you to feel loyal to our brand? Would you buy our product tomorrow if you had a need?
- What do we do well?
- Where can we improve?

Many companies will wait for a service failure or other event to survey the customer. While it's important to get timely customer perceptions of service, during or just after an event, this should not be the only time you ask them to rate services if you are honestly looking to improve customer loyalty and satisfaction. This is because, besides the emotion that may be involved with a part failure, you may also be asking for money to perform the repairs. These things put the customer in a defensive position, and you are unlikely to get insightful information about your business.

The best time to gather customer information regarding field service expectations is in the course of talking about new products. Ask the customer the following:

- What services do you want to go along with the product?
- What do you need to know in advance, before deploying the product?
- Will you need on-site field service engineers if the product fails?
- Is product uptime business critical?
- Do you need redundant capability?
- What should other people in the organization have input into the services wants and needs discussion? Business people? Engineering? Technical people? Operations?

Field service managers can be helpful when assisting the salespeople in describing the field service capabilities of the company. This may open up a whole new selling avenue and penetration of the customer organization.

We always caution field service organizations not to make assumptions about customers. You must take the time and make the effort to ask.

4 Form Customer Advisory Boards to Build Loyalty

Invite and engage your top 20% and your most strategic customers to the CAB.

A Customer Advisory Board (CAB) can be a real asset. This is especially true for field service; if it is conducted to achieve goals you have in mind and is organized in a professional way. So what can you expect from a CAB?

- Identification of changing customer needs and emerging opportunities
- Market direction information to feed your product and service development
- Information on industry trends that may apply to your customers
- Intelligence on competitors' offerings
- Early warning signs of issues with your products or services
- Good will and loyalty from participating customers
- Significant new revenue from ideas spawned through discussion

Customers, no matter their size and importance to you, want to be heard, especially when they have important topics to discuss. The CAB is a forum for discussion with your company representatives to address topics in a non-crisis environment.

Invite your top 20% customers, in terms of revenue, to the CAB. Also invite strategic customers who are influential in their industry or have unique situations to address. Invite your executives to participate, and make sure they commit to staying all day and socialize during breaks and lunch. Make this an all-day planned event with lunch and coffee breaks provided, so you have time to talk informally with customers and build relationships. When the event is over, debrief with your executives, and learn what they discovered.

Most CABs include 10–20 people. If you go over that number of participants, it will be difficult to handle discussions. It's better to have a smaller group where everyone participates but not so small that not enough new ideas are generated. Choose discussion topics that will be engaging and relevant so that the participation level is high.

Companies generally do not compensate customers for participation in CABs; however, it is customary to provide meals during the meeting and, sometimes, hotel accommodations.

Designate one or two people from your staff to take careful notes at the event. Have them capture as much information as possible including who said what and the context within which it was said. Capture suggestions on flip charts or whiteboards. Some companies may hire a professional meeting consultant to assist with managing the event.

Set the expectation for the CAB with your staff and stakeholders. Keep your own company participants well informed about the schedule and agenda. Set expectations for participants by inviting them well in advance (six to eight weeks), sending an advance agenda, and reviewing it at the start of the day. Some of the expectations may include openness and honesty in discussion and feedback, full attention (perhaps no cell phones or laptops), help with an action plan for each item, and willingness to continue to participate in problem resolution or testing of new solutions.

Warning: Do not allow the CAB to be used for customers to publically vent their anger about something that has happened or a problem with your equipment. Make sure that major issues have been discussed and solved with this customer prior to their attendance at the CAB, or make arrangements to have this customer meet in private with executives and engineers who can take action to help.

Most importantly, follow up with participants regarding what your company is doing to change and improve field service as a result of their participation. Joe Pinto, SVP Technical Service at Cisco, hosts several CABs per year. He stresses, "The worst thing you can do is ask for feedback and then not do anything." You want to keep these most important customers well informed and engaged in the process. You will be rewarded by loyal customers who are advocates for your company.

5 Know the Competition to Avoid Surprises

We are wired. We can search topics, brands, and business issues pretty much anytime, anywhere in the world. If your customer wants to know about your company or your competitors, he or she can do some fast online research. This environment makes keeping up with what the competition is offering easy to research but hard for you to compete against. Things move fast. We have to be on our toes, be aware at all times, and make good use of the information at our fingertips (or thumbs if we use a smartphone!)

We recommend field service departments electronically scan the competitive horizon regularly, at least monthly. This scan should include the following activities for your top competitors every month and all competitors annually:

- Review competitors' web site for updates, new offerings, and changes.
- Review annual reports, 10Ks, and other financial documents for comments on service offerings, revenues, and profitability.
- Google search for articles on competitors' field service capabilities.
- Search industry web sites such as Field Technologies and Aberdeen Group.
- Attend professional industry events.
- Attend field service trade shows and conferences.

In addition to web-based research and attendance at industry events, another way to find out what's happening in the competitive market is to talk to customers. Your salespeople should be asking your customers what they like and dislike about your services and about your competitors' services. Carefully record information gathered in this way for your competitive analysis. Here is an example: When doing business in India, Jim Reily asked customers about field support, and they complained loudly about delays and part shortages. Easy solution is to add field inventory. But before executing an expensive inventory build-out and depot expansion plan, Jim asked further about how his company compared with the competition. The customers uniformly noted that his support was far better than any competitors. So, Jim improved support capabilities but in a measured way and only when generating additional service revenue to offset the expense.

Enlist the support of your marketing department to conduct a formal marketplace survey. If crafted correctly, these surveys can be a wealth of information regarding how your products and services are viewed in the market. Get your legal department to review the survey, so you can be sure the questions you ask are appropriate.

Establish a customer advisory council where customers give you feedback and suggestions about products and services. If you already have a council established, consider expanding it to include field service, new service products, and what customers like and don't like about you and your competitors' service. See Rule 4 for more details on customer advisory boards.

Understand what competitors say they are doing, and then determine if they are actually performing and whether the services provide competitive advantage in the marketplace. You will find that web site information is often written by marketing professionals who don't really understand field service operations. The language used may be very appealing to customers but may not correctly represent services offered.

Any information that is publically available on a web site, in brochures, from a trade fair, in articles written and published, or in presentations made to a public audience is fair game. We do not advocate obtaining any private or proprietary information, no matter how valuable it may seem.

Your competitors may have developed some new service that will become their competitive advantage. If so, you must consider developing a similar offering, or you may lose market share. You should also be able to glean a development path from competitive information, which will act as input for your own company field service strategy.

There's a very old saying, "Keep your friends close and your enemies closer" (Sun Tzu, Chinese general and military strategist, ~400 BC).

6 Win Against Competitors by Servicing Their Products or Not

Goldmine or quagmire?

Should your field service team fix competitor's products? The question comes up frequently in field service organizations and is often raised by field service engineers (FSE). Here is the situation: Your FSE can see that some other manufacturer's equipment needs repair or must be tweaked to work in conjunction with your equipment. The customer asks for help, and your people are willing and confident that they can do the repairs. If your FSEs know the equipment and you have the parts, why not?

On the plus side, you satisfy a customer, you increase service revenue, you increase utilization of your FSEs, and, more important, you may have an opportunity to replace competitors' equipment with your equipment in the future. On the minus side, you may need to train on their equipment and buy their parts. You may not have access to escalation engineers if you hit a really tough problem.

Aggressive field service managers identify potential streams of revenue coming from offering a broad range of repair services on equipment from different manufacturers. Take appliance repair, for example. If you call a repairman to service your dishwasher or air conditioner, typically, he can service many makes and models. The same is true for auto repair shops, watch repair, and others. In these cases, service training and repair parts are widely available, so there is a wide choice of companies offering service beyond the original manufacturer.

By contrast, complex industrial equipment is more challenging to service properly. Your field team will need extensive training and may require certification to work on a product. Parts may be expensive and only available from the original manufacturer. Many manufacturers prefer to have only their repair people service their equipment, so training may not be available at all. Some companies protect against outside service providers by warning the customer that the warranty will be null and void if the equipment is serviced by others.

Consider these factors when deciding to service other manufacturer's equipment:

- Can you procure training necessary to provide superior service for this equipment?
- Do you have a reliable source of quality parts, at reasonable prices?
- Can you procure special tools or diagnostic equipment needed?
- Can you get latest technical documentation?
- How will you be notified and deal with product safety issues, engineering, and field change orders?
- How will you deal with warranty issues?
- What is your strategy to deal with troubleshooting issues your FSEs can't solve?
- When you consider costs, can you price service competitively?
- What is your strategy to replace competitor's equipment with your equipment; consider timing, price incentives, and long-term service contracts?

Perhaps, the biggest benefit is that your field service people will collect knowledge about features and benefits that your equipment may not have. Survey your field service people regularly to collect this important field intelligence, and feed it back to your own product development and marketing departments.

It doesn't have to be win or lose; one approach to consider is to form a partnership with other manufacturers. This is what's known as "co-opetition."[1]

Jack Welch, the former CEO of GE, was famous for recommending that GE field service people work on everyone's equipment. Jack was convinced that by doing so, not only would GE make money, but they would also gain extremely valuable insight about their competitors, including opportunities to replace competitors' equipment with GE equipment.

Ultimately, if you have an underutilized field team; can secure the training, parts, and engineering documentation; and, most important, have willing customers, you can benefit greatly by servicing other manufacturer's equipment.

---

1. Basic principles of co-opetitive structures have been described in game theory, a scientific field that received more attention with the book *Theory of Games and Economic Behavior* in 1944 and the works of John Forbes Nash, Jr., on *Non-cooperative Games.*

7 Meet Specific Industry and Customer Needs

One size does NOT fit all.

To deliver superior service, you must understand key drivers in your customer's industries and how your equipment adds value. Not all field services are standard "break/fix." Customers in oil and gas will have service needs varying widely from customers in retail or the airline industry. Although they all may use the same or similar versions of your equipment, their service needs must be individually addressed.

Most successful service organizations market and perform ranges of service offerings. Cisco Systems Inc., for instance, developed a comprehensive set of service offerings, called PPDIOO, that address the full lifecycle of the product. PPDIOO (which stands for Prepare, Plan, Design, Implement, Operate, and Optimize) offers service modules tailored to specific customer and industry needs. Customers choose bundles or individual modules to support their specific operational requirements and budgets.

A common example of segmentation and bundling is the airline industry with their bundles of First Class, Business Class and Economy flight services. Each bundle includes basic transportation with higher-value bundles enhanced by type of seating, boarding priority, food and beverage service, etc. Customers purchasing the Economy bundle can also choose individual additional "modules" such as food service, alcoholic beverages, and baggage service. These "modules" are offered for additional cost above basic Economy bundle price.

If your products are mission critical to your customer, they must have very high reliability, and your service products must support this requirement. For example, train traffic monitoring systems, air traffic control, Wall Street trading networks, and hospital systems all require very high uptime. Telco networks, such as AT&T, strive to achieve 99.9999% reliability (uptime). This translates to an outage of just 31 seconds per year. Telco companies often buy redundant equipment and demand service response within a one- to two-hour window to fix any broken equipment so they maintain at least one level of redundancy.

Dentists and other small businesses may require high levels of uptime, too. If the vacuum system or autoclave in a dental office goes down, the office must shut down until the equipment is fixed. On the other hand, if one of the several dental chairs breaks, the dental office may be able to get by with the other three chairs for 24–72 hours until a repairman arrives.

To determine the level of criticality of your service products, you must segregate customers by industry and by how your equipment is being used by your customer. Starting with this analysis, think about the service components you can bundle to meet the needs of the customer. Determine how this bundle may be different by industry. For example, the hospital industry bundle of services will probably be different from the automotive bundle. While they may all use your products, their needs must be individually addressed. Differentiating gives you strategic advantage over competitors that simply offer generic alternatives. It can also deliver better margins as higher-value service commands higher pricing.

"One size does not fit all. We have tiered parts support plans that offer immediate delivery, 2–3 days delivery and 6–8 weeks delivery, priced accordingly. The most important thing is to set the right customer expectation," says Michel Yasso of MSR Consulting Group.

Within each industry, you should segregate operations by criticality. Consider airlines again: If you fly First Class, you expect priority boarding, your coat hung up when you are seated, more comfortable seating, and to be served food and liquor, all with a smile and friendly attitude from the best flight attendants. This is the special service you can expect when you pay the premium First Class price. When you pay for an Economy ticket, you expect and receive less.

8 Field Service Is Critical To Your Brand

Keep customers coming back again and again for new products.

The American Marketing Association defines a brand as a "name, term, design, symbol, or any other feature that identifies one seller's good or service as distinct from those of other sellers."

Your company brand is a valuable asset. The reputation of your brand depends on the quality of products and the services provided. The Nordstrom brand is famous for all of the anecdotal stories about their exceptional customer service. Service is key to Nordstrom's reputation and brand and, over the years, has created fierce customer loyalty.

Brands enable consumers to form expectations about a company. Brand value is all around us every day and contributes to our choices in products. Take Tylenol vs. a store's generic brand: Generally, we perceive the Tylenol brand to have more value and thus command a higher price even though the drug formulation may be identical to the generic. We actually pay more for a brand with a good reputation. And customers' paying more translates into better margins for the business.

In the industrial products and electronic equipment world, fast and effective service is dependent on uptime. Businesses depend on having their networks and production running all the time. Equipment failures cause panic, but if your service response is fast and solves the problem efficiently, your customers will assign more value to your brand.

The great brand reputations of the world are closely guarded by their owners. They understand that branding is not only about getting current customers to continue to choose you over the competition. It is also about getting your prospects to see you as the company that provides the best solution to their problem. To build this kind of brand recognition and respect takes time and focused effort. Your reputation for fast, efficient, and high-quality service will win many customers and keep them coming back over many years.

Your brand resides within the hearts and minds of existing and prospective customers. It is the sum total of their experiences and perceptions with your company whether through direct experience, word-of-mouth referrals, or advertising. So what can field service organizations do to enhance brand reputation? Here is a list of field service "must dos" to protect and build your brand:

- Respond to all phone calls within the time promised (typically within one hour).
- Have knowledgeable people in the call center who can help diagnose the problem, not just note takers.
- Send well-trained and qualified people into the field to solve problems and repair equipment.
- Send field service representatives (FSRs) and field service engineers (FSEs) who are friendly, fast, and efficient and who clean up after themselves.
- Err on the side of the customer being right. Don't make the customer fight for services from you.
- Check on customer satisfaction regularly. If you need to make corrections, do it swiftly.
- Never hesitate on safety issues. Make sure everyone understands that safety is always first.
- Advertise your emphasis on service, and get customer endorsements whenever possible.

Ultimately, the quality of your field service will impact the value of your brand. "Siemens has a good reputation for quality and service in the field," says Christine Parlett, Services Director, Siemens Strategy and Business Development. "Siemens has set up a totally new division for Services. Service organizations are not just part of the manufacturing sites anymore. This is an important step in raising the importance of Service to our customers and within the Siemens organization. Siemens is building a strong customer service profile."

Positive branding regarding field service will not only affect initial product purchases by your customer, but it will also keep customers coming back again and again for new products in the future.

9 Develop the Perfect Services for the Perfect Customer

If you had the perfect customer, what would that be like?

As consultants, we often lead our clients through a Vision Workshop called "The Perfect Customer." The purpose of such a workshop (usually one to two hours) is to open up the discussion and think creatively about what could be possible in a perfect world. This leads to a discussion regarding potential new services, communication enhancements, and other topics that could work perfectly every time, for your perfect customer. Most companies find that this exercise helps to define the behaviors you really want from customers and, in order to get these behaviors, what level of service you must provide. Because we have so few opportunities in day-to-day business to be creative, most people find the visualization workshop to be a valuable and fun exercise.

Conducting the Workshop

Let's start with the perfect customer who has unlimited funds to spend on service. If this were the case, would your company provide top-of-the-line spares? Although more expensive, do these spares last longer and therefore have to be replaced less often in the field? If less time is required in the field, are there savings to be achieved? Perhaps, a review of the spares, focusing on reliability and longevity may bring you to the conclusion that you should upgrade all your spare parts. The Vision Workshop is not the place to discuss this in detail. It is the place to generate lots of good ideas, however, just like this one.

Next, let's think about communication. If your perfect customer could communicate the need for service via any means, what is your preferred method? Phone? E-mail? Automated Internet transaction? How far in advance would you prefer to receive this communication? If you knew, for example, that your customer would need a service call in two weeks and that request would be communicated automatically, would that help you? Today, to achieve this perfect situation, many high-tech companies are adding self-diagnostic software into their equipment. This software communicates via cellular technology or the Internet to warn of an impending service failure. Companies can schedule maintenance well in advance of a failure, and it can be done electronically, thus reducing the need for call center personnel and frustrated customers with broken products. Make a note to investigate this later, and move on to more visioning.

You may think that customers with a great attitude may be a rarity in the field service world, but are they really? Your perfect customer in a perfect world is probably cheerful, patient, understanding, and grateful. How do you change current customer behavior to perfect customer behavior? Perhaps, there is customer service or call center training to improve the way conversations go between customers and your customer service people. Perhaps, systems enhancements would speed answers to customers. What else can you dream of to help your perfect customer respond cheerfully and patiently? Could you provide faster service? Could you improve FSE's interaction with them?

As always in business, you should consider new ways to increase revenue. In a perfect world, your perfect customer would spend unlimited dollars on services they found were a good value and beneficial to them. So what are some ways to help your perfect customer spend more? Perhaps, spending more time selling service contracts when equipment is purchased is one way to increase revenues. Emphasizing the benefits of your products every time your customer is on the phone is another way. Teach your customer service people to sell.

As long as ideas are free flowing in the Vision Workshop, keep on going. Capture as many new ideas as possible, and help everyone understand the vision of perfect services for perfect customers.

So now that you have a lot of great ideas, what's next? In order to turn these into reality, you must prioritize by impact on revenue/margin and customer satisfaction. You can do this with the group or with a subset of the team knowledgeable about the "big picture" of your business. Then pick top-value ideas, assign them to appropriate groups, and have ideas "fleshed out" to projects with specific benefits and costs. Start the most promising projects.

10 Field Service Is Not Just "Break/Fix"

Think big: Swing for the fences.

How do you define field service?

We advocate thinking big and "swinging for the fences" as they say in baseball. Not only should you be responding to customer repairs and providing ongoing maintenance, there is more that you can offer to add value for your customer and increase your revenues.

For example, companies such as General Electric that produce large equipment for power generation offer to conduct a site evaluation prior to delivering equipment to the installation to ensure a smooth and successful install. Field service can provide practical and valuable consulting assistance to customers on all aspects of the layout and site design, as well as the requirements for optimal operation of equipment. These valuable consulting services can command substantial consulting fees. Services such as these can also be serious differentiators when selling equipment. Your field service people know what's best, based on experience, and you can charge for this expertise.

Cisco considers consulting part of its "PPDIOO" customer cycle and offers services that span the lifecycle for networking technologies. These services are provided by its own workforce and service partners. This consists of the following steps in the customer cycle:

- *Prepare*: discovery process to define customer business needs
- *Plan*: site and solution requirement definition
- *Design*: development of implementation design
- *Implement*: installation of equipment to meet business needs

- **Operate:** transition to routine operation
- **Optimize:** continuous system improvement and optimization

Consulting fees can be charged for processes such as Cisco's PPDIOO and can make a huge difference to your bottom line. At each step in the process, you engage with your customer to gain a deeper understanding of their goals. This, in turn, will enable you to make helpful recommendations.

If you decide to include consulting services in your field service organization, you will need to develop some standardized approaches and deliverables, just as you would expect from any professional consulting organization. This might include an audit document and checklist for use by field service consultants for site visits and consultations and a standardized deliverable report template to be given to your customer. Be sure to make these documents standardized. In fact, you will need higher-skilled engineers for the more strategic work. Remember, if the customer is paying for this work, they will expect professional deliverables that are insightful, well written, and polished.

Fees for consulting work can vary depending on the expertise required for the project. The typical range is $1,200–2,000 per day. These prices are competitive with consultants across all disciplines in the USA. Fees in other countries may be higher or lower depending on the norms for that country. Fees for very technical or programming work may command even higher rates. Remember, consulting involves strategic as well as tactical work, commanding a higher level of compensation.

Customers will willingly pay your fees if they find significant value in the results. Some of our clients use consulting work as a front-end loss leader if they think they can close a deal for equipment and ongoing maintenance as a result of this work. In these cases, there is no charge for the initial consulting work or a credit against the equipment invoice if the customer proceeds with the purchase.

Many companies are moving from reactive "break/fix" to proactive "intelligent" services that utilize advances in diagnostics and Internet connectivity to forecast service needs or optimization potential at the equipment level. Joe Pinto, SVP at Cisco, believes "companies can't rest on their laurels." Joe uses proactive "smart services" to help drive reductions in the cost of operations (COO) and improve the value of the product for the customer's business.

There is a home run out there in customer satisfaction and increased revenue if you think of field service as more than "break/fix."

Part II
Operations

Operations are the foundation for delivering superior field service. In this section, we will help you prepare for natural and man-made disasters, understand the value of Key Performance Indicators (KPIs), show the impact of Engineering Change Orders, and see the importance of reverse logistics, going green, and maintaining an accurate installed base. We highlight the use of computing the cost of downtime, the risk of counterfeit parts, and the need for critical, honest feedback in field service performance and the necessity to have a road map for your service organization. Following these rules will help you achieve operational excellence and deliver superior field service.

Operations Rules:

- Rule 11: Shit Happens—Plan Ahead and Be Prepared
- Rule 12: You Can't Get What You Don't Measure
- Rule 13: Engineering Change Orders Can Be Field Service Financial Disasters
- Rule 14: Pay Attention to Returns
- Rule 15: Help Customers Determine the Cost of Downtime
- Rule 16: Consider Outsourcing
- Rule 17: It's Good to Be Green
- Rule 18: Build and Maintain Accurate Installed Base Data
- Rule 19: Train Your Teams to Deal with Counterfeits
- Rule 20: Field Service Feedback Is Essential for New and Improved Products
- Rule 21: To Get Where You Are Going, You Need a Road Map

11 Shit Happens—Plan Ahead and Be Prepared

Have a recovery plan ready to assist customers when disaster strikes.

Disasters are going to happen, and you need to be prepared. In addition to natural disasters such as fires, earthquakes, floods, volcanoes, and hurricanes (referred to as force majeure), we also must be prepared for man-made events such as the terrorist attacks on 9/11.

Natural disasters around the world require that you plan for events in global locations where your equipment may reside. The US Geological Survey says, "There is a two out of three chance that a 6.7-magnitude or larger earthquake will happen in the Bay Area within the next 30 years. A quake of this size would be significantly damaging and would impact our lives for days if not weeks."

The United States National Counterterrorism Center (NCTC) Report on Terrorism published in March 2010 states, "Approximately 11,000 terrorist attacks occurred in 83 countries during 2009, resulting in over 58,000 victims, including nearly 15,000 fatalities."

On September 11, 2001, companies had to respond to the emergency situation after the collapse of the World Trade Center towers and the crash into the Pentagon. Cisco's field service organization immediately swung into action and set up a command center to respond to the events. Cisco Field Service, Sales and Partners helped several trading firms reconstitute themselves with VoIP in alternate locations such as New Jersey. Concurrently, Cisco dispatched additional trucks with service parts and systems to the impacted sites, to rapidly repair the damage and get the customers back in business.

Advanced planning and practice drills prepared Cisco service for fast response. Being prepared and practicing for such events is a key component to providing superior field service.

Here are the things to consider when planning for or responding to any disaster:

1. **Highest priority:** Check on your people—Is everyone accounted for? Are they safe? Do they need assistance? Can they help you service customers?
2. Activate a command center and your emergency plan to manage the response.
3. Determine who can assess the situation at the site(s). How will you communicate with them?
4. Determine how quickly you can return to business. Was there damage to the facilities?
5. Determine what it will take to get your service and your customers back up and running.
6. Determine if you need to engage emergency partners. Do we have contract technicians available?
7. Assess the availability of air transport. If not available, can you get trucks into the area? Do you have nearby spares depots?
8. Determine if you need passes or permits to get into the area.
9. Coordinate with local, state, and federal government agencies.
10. Determine how customers will contact you. Do you have additional phone and Internet response people in place?

There are many scenarios in disaster planning, and you should be prepared for several kinds of responses. The response to a power outage or a severe storm is different from a terrorist attack. Your planning should include several types of responses, concentrating on those most likely to occur.

Budgeting is also a very important component to your ability to respond. Be sure to engage executive management in advanced planning discussions regarding budgeting and decision-making authority delegation. When a disaster happens, you won't have time to talk to the CFO about money or the COO about making operational decisions.

Planning for disasters and conducting drills to test those plans may seem like a low priority when faced with the pressures of daily operations. If you make the time to do this, you will be richly rewarded by grateful, more loyal customers when you help them keep their businesses operating after disaster strikes.

12 You Can't Get What You Don't Measure

Key Performance Indicators can help manage your business.

If you aren't using Key Performance Indicators (KPIs) to manage field service, you should start now. If you are using KPIs, align these measures with your company business strategy, and review them regularly to ensure they are synched with business goals. You will get the behavior you want from measuring things you focus on.

To improve customer satisfaction and loyalty, you must generate customer-meaningful KPIs; measuring what customers determine is most important to their business, not what you think is important. Typically, these include product uptime, first-time fix, MTTR (meantime to repair), and MTBF (meantime between failures). While equipment uptime is the best measure of overall product reliability and field service quality, Morris Cohen of the Wharton School noted, "For many customers, first time fix is the most important metric for field service quality."

Other internal measures, such as cost per repair and inventory to revenue ratio, are used to manage effectiveness and efficiency of your business.

While it may seem obvious that talking with your customers is a good idea, the politics of some companies may dictate that only salespeople can talk to customers. You may have to convince Sales that you need to speak with customers directly. But you must collect what customers think are the right measures in order to improve and build customer satisfaction and loyalty.

World-class companies, like Ford and GM, utilize third-party customer surveys to determine overall satisfaction and dissatisfaction with product and service performance. Employee compensation is tied to achieving customer satisfaction goals. John Chambers, CEO of Cisco Systems Inc., has said, "Customer satisfaction is a personal top priority and I fully expect it to be a top priority of everyone who works at Cisco."[2]

Most companies capture and measure feedback after a field service call or phone call. This idea has been popularized by groups such as auto service departments, banks, and telecom. This relentless collection of information is used to drive service improvements. Customers appreciate having a voice and will give valuable feedback when service is below expectations. When service is superior, you gain customer loyalty.

You should consider having KPIs by customer. Individual KPIs may be harder to manage, but they will be more meaningful, especially for large and profitable customers. Advances in ERP and CRM systems allow you to generate customer-specific KPIs with minimum additional cost.

Here are some common KPIs:

- Equipment uptime: most important overall KPI. Definitions vary by customer (i.e., "SEMI e-10" is a standard measure for the semiconductor industry). Very high-uptime requirements (such as telephone companies) will require equipment redundancy or on-site parts and technicians.
- First-time fix: Was equipment fixed correctly the first time?
- Service response time: customers may say they want 7x24 coverage but only want to pay for 5x12 service.
- MTTR (meantime to repair)
- MTBF (meantime between failure)
- SOFR (service order fill rate): Were you able to deliver all parts needed for repair?
- LIFR (line item fill rate): internal measure to determine effectiveness of your inventory planning systems
- Distribution quality: right parts at the right place
- Customer satisfaction after repair: How satisfied are they with the service?
- Ratio between planned maintenance and corrective maintenance: this ratio should be ~90 to 100.
- Field engineer utilization: amount of time the service person is generating revenue based on 2088 hours/year/person less vacation/training/holidays
- Cost per repair action by product line and geography
- Service inventory efficiency such as value of inventory vs. service revenue or value of inventory vs. value of installed base of product supported. We recommend you avoid inventory turns to measure service inventory (see Rule 26).

---

2. *John Chambers and the Cisco Way: Navigating Through Volatility* by John Kevin Waters. John Wiley & Sons.

13

Engineering Change Orders Can Be Field Service Financial Disasters

Oops, did that change cause a field service problem?

Ahhh, the darling of twenty-first-century automobiles, the Prius, caused a lot of grief for Toyota and garnered a very public apology from the company chairman, when the brakes on some cars failed. Repairs to the faulty brake systems reportedly cost Toyota US$ 2 billion.[3] A simple change to the design in manufacturing (before the vehicles left the production line) could have saved the $2 billion and the reputation of Toyota. When repairs must be done after product is deployed to the field, costs are magnified, and brand reputation is hurt (see Rule 8).

Of course, when field changes are required for safety reasons, they are necessary. But too often, we find our clients making other engineering changes without ever considering the cost to complete changes in the field.

In the manufacturing world, it is common to have up to 30% of the product changed through engineering change orders (ECOs) each year. Further, another 10% may be due to something that must be changed or fixed as a field change order (FCO). Most companies don't consider the full financial impact of field service. But world-class companies do.

World-class companies design products with service in mind. This is commonly known as "design for serviceability." In the product design process, the product goes through a complete review by the field service organization. In this review, all parts of the product are considered for potential repair processes, meantime between

---

3. Forbes.com Kelsey Swanekamp, 02.04.10, 12:15 PM EST

failure (MTBF), and meantime to repair (MTTR) of the total product as well as subassemblies and individual parts. Product quality may also be involved to review the overall product quality strategy. There must be final sign-off by the involved departments and partners before the product can go into production. World-class companies also develop written repair procedures for field engineers or other repair partners before a new product is released. The same processes are followed for new ECOs. If an ECO triggers field repairs, then additional repair instructions must be written to support the changes.

It is important to keep in mind that the customer doesn't typically pay for field changes, ECOs, or FCOs. This additional expense to your company should be included in the total cost of the product. In addition to field labor repair expense, the cost of additional inventory for repairs and logistics costs, such as global sourcing and customs duties on parts, must be considered. Moreover, product organizations will want to minimize costs to them by recommending, for example, that field inventory of old or down rev service parts be used up rather than replaced with the new improved parts. Don't believe them; as soon as customers find out that newer better parts are available, they will demand to have new parts used for any equipment repairs.

Antennaegate

When the iPhone4 lost its signal when it was held in a certain way, Apple offered to provide a free case to every iPhone4 owner. Steve Jobs, Apple CEO, held a press conference to announce the case offering, apologized for the product failure, and explained what steps the company was taking to correct the problem.

In the meantime, the issue caused a blogging frenzy dubbed "Antennaegate." Shares of Apple, the world's biggest technology company by market value, fell $1.61 to $260.09 on August 6, 2010, in response to the announcement.[4]

Not only was this an expensive field repair, but Apple suffered in reputation and lost significant market valuation. The people responsible for this failure left the company.

So be cautious—you may decide not to make the change based on the financial impact. The costs need to be balanced against customer dissatisfaction and marketplace perception.

---

4. Bloomberg: *Apple's IPhone Executive Mark Papermaster Leaves After Antenna Complaints* by Arik Hesseldahl. August 8, 2010, 7:27 AM PT.

14 Pay Attention to Returns

RMA numbers are essential to the returns process.

Returns and reverse logistics are challenging. Customers consider returns low value and low priority. But the financial impact to your business of getting products and parts back quickly and efficiently can be huge.

Getting that part returned is very important and valuable to you. The part may be repairable and could be resold as refurbished equipment. It may also be important to your quality engineering people in evaluating defects and failures. And you want to keep equipment away from secondary markets to protect your IP and avoid it being sold as used equipment. Dillard Myers, VP of Global Service Supply Chain at Cisco Systems Inc., notes, "Returned parts are crucial to our ability to provide excellent service to our customers while keeping costs down."

To reclaim these parts and information about defects, implement a process that includes easy customer returns and active receiving and evaluation processing at your return facility. In addition, give your customer an incentive for expediting the return. Many companies initiate a replacement invoice for warranty or repair items. When a broken or damaged part is returned, the customer's invoice is credited. If the broken part is not returned, the customer is billed.

Dell Computer guarantees laptop parts if you buy an extended warranty. Let's say, for example, that your keyboard malfunctions and needs to be replaced. Dell will send you a keyboard, but only after you send in the old one first. If you insist, they may send you the replacement part before you return the broken one but only if you give Dell your credit card number and agree to be charged if they do not receive the broken one back.

Return Material Authorization or RMA numbers are critical to processing parts. The RMA number is usually associated with the original order number so warranty costs and serialization can be tracked. In this way, returned material can be tracked, and defect origins identified. The equipment being serviced should also be tracked to validate that the warranty or service contract is active. Your quality department may want to trace the part to your vendors or correlate defects with other similar defective parts. In addition, when parts are returned, they can be easily identified and set on the path for repair or quality examination.

We have a client that could not associate a returned part to a warranty time frame. Their customer service call center assigned an RMA number to anything the customer wanted to return then fixed or replaced the part, without knowing if it was under warranty or not. Our client simply did not have the systems in place to determine this information, so they gave away all repairs for free! With a systems implementation, we helped them change this process and begin to charge for repairs beyond the warranty period.

Once the item arrives at your repair facility, a process should be followed for dispositioning the part. Your process should include the following:

- Receiving RMA part
- Matching RMA number to customer order number and serial number of newly installed replacement part
- Identifying serial number and updating installed base with removed or replaced serial numbers
- Examining part for defects, recording description of problem or defect as indicated by customer or field service, and disposition of part for evaluation or repair
- Processing part expeditiously to get it back into inventory for resale or use or determining potential defect and safety issues

Returns or reverse logistics operations are usually given a very low priority for talent and resources; don't make this mistake. Returned parts and products are an excellent source of material for refurbishment and use in field service. They contain valuable information on product failures, and they contain your valuable intellectual property. Make good use of this "golden" resource.

15 Help Customers Determine the Cost of Downtime

Convince your customer to sign up for a higher level of service because of the high cost of downtime.

Most companies don't have a good understanding of what downtime really costs. This is probably because downtime creates an emergency situation and people get busy trying to resolve the emergency. The actual cost is never calculated. Here are the categories to be considered as part of downtime costs:

- Rescheduling costs on the shop floor, labor, and overtime
- Loss of work time: employees productivity if they must stop work to wait for repairs
- Damaged work if a machine or process failure causes quality issues
- Loss revenue or sales due to late deliveries
- Customer satisfaction and loyalty: for example, Aircraft On Ground or "AOG" causing flight delay or cancellation
- Use of premium transportation
- Potential legal liabilities
- Emergency services costs
- Impact to your brand

Smart customers will sign up for higher levels of service because they understand the high cost of downtime. Typically, service products come in multiple levels such as silver, gold, and platinum which correlate to low, medium, and high service responsiveness. To find the best match of service to your customer needs, help your customers understand the total cost of downtime correlated with the levels of service. If their downtime cost is high, they will be more likely to buy a higher level of service.

Mission-critical systems may not only require high service levels but also redundant equipment, so there is virtually no overall system downtime. Businesses such as hospitals, hotels, and transportation companies require backup generators to keep operations going, no matter what happens. Of course, no one can predict natural disasters, terrorist strikes, and other terrible events that may cause outages that cannot be planned.

If your company has global customers, they may demand prompt recovery or take their business elsewhere. Jim Miller, VP of Operations at Google, confirms, "A Google outage is just not acceptable. We have multiple levels of redundancy and service support to ensure we are up continuously."

In other cases, the customer may not be willing to provide total cost of downtime because it is considered confidential or competitive in nature. Software companies are reluctant to give out any server-related downtime even if it is for scheduled maintenance. This is because competitors will pick up this information and use it against them in competitive sales situations. Research In Motion or RIM, the operator of the Blackberry network, for example, suffered a network outage that prevented their customers from getting e-mail for several days. Many customers jumped ship for Apple iPhones. Unfortunately, RIM never fully recovered and is now struggling to stay in business.

Closer to home, you have probably experienced cable, Internet, or satellite outages from time to time. These periods can be incredibly frustrating, especially if you have to wait for ordinary service. If you could pay for immediate response and get your home networks back up immediately, would you?

We admire Eliyhu Goldratt's body of work[5] regarding pinch points and bottlenecks in supply chains. Goldratt recommends that if equipment is on the critical path for manufacturing, then plan for alternate approaches including alternate pathways for production, redundant systems, and tight timeframe service-level agreements (SLAs). We couldn't agree more, and your service organization should address these ideas with customers.

High levels of service response time cost more in terms of a customer's service contract but are less expensive than downtime. For one of our clients, we calculated the downtime for a semiconductor chip manufacturing line to be well over $40,000 per hour.

So help your customers determine the cost of downtime, and use that cost to justify a field service package that minimizes their overall costs.

---

5. *The Goal: A Process of Ongoing Improvement* by Eliyhu Goldratt.

16 Consider Outsourcing

If field service is a core competency, consider providing service for other companies.

If you walk into a Verizon store and need to have your phone serviced, you will be greeted by a friendly, well-trained service person, willing to assist you. What you may not realize is that this service person is not a Verizon employee but part of an outsourced service organization. Verizon has made the decision to focus on selling phones and operating a cellular network.

Many of our clients have chosen to outsource the servicing of their equipment and just focus on their primary business whether it is manufacturing, networking, or retailing. You should think about outsourcing as this may provide an enormous opportunity for you. You could outsource your own service department and just provide management and oversight. Or you could offer outsourcing to other companies and provide field service for their equipment.

Let's examine outsourcing your own field service first. The initial questions to ask are "What are our core competencies?" and "What capabilities does our company have that give us a competitive advantage?" If field service is not at least part of the answer to these questions, then you should consider outsourcing. If another company can execute field service better than you, then it may be a wise business decision to evaluate alternatives. There are plenty of examples where field service outsourcing is common and established channel partners such as Choice, Flash, Ryder, UPS, FedEx, Pro Logistics, and Glass House are servicing equipment worldwide.

Another option may be to maintain your field service operations such as management, training, and dispatch but outsource the field service representatives or use independent contractors. You can still maintain control over training, certification, and performance without taking on additional employee overhead. Many field service people prefer being contractors to take advantage of a more flexible work schedule.

If your company provides best-in-class field service and it is considered part of your core competency and a competitive advantage, then you should consider providing services to other companies. In an article published by the Wharton School of Business "Power by the Hour" describes an emerging trend particularly in aerospace and defense. The term "Power by the Hour" was coined by Rolls-Royce in the 1990s to describe their performance-based contracts for engines and other avionics products that were sold to commercial airlines. Today, "engine manufacturers General Electric, Pratt & Whitney, and Rolls-Royce all have performance-based contracts with commercial airlines in which their compensation is tied to product availability (hours flown)," the authors write in their study.[6] This has resulted in a profitable business for GE and a cost reduction for the airlines (win–win).

Providing outsourcing to your customers and even your competitors can take on many forms. But no matter what direction you take, make absolutely sure you have considered every detail before you transition to an outsource model. This means that every process should be documented and agreed to by both companies. Training requirements and certifications must be in place. Escalation procedures and response times should be fully determined and agreed to. Payment schedules and services fees must be in writing. All these things and more must be part of the contract between you and your outsource partner company. The transition timeline should be documented in detail and carefully managed. Remember, if there are problems with the transition and customer service falters as a result, you will be jeopardizing revenues.

Outsourcing is a powerful way to leverage your core competencies or take advantage of other partners' strengths to compliment your services. Done well, it increases your customer satisfaction, profitability, and competitive advantage. Done poorly, you will have a long road to recovery.

---

6. *"Power by the Hour": Can Paying Only for Performance Redefine How Products Are Sold and Serviced?* Knowledge at Wharton. http://knowledge.wharton.upenn.edu/article.cfm?articleid=1665.

17 It's Good to Be Green

Good stewardship has important ramifications for your company's market performance.

Good stewardship over your products and how your company affects the environment not only makes your company a good corporate citizen but also has important ramifications for your market performance. A study published in the summer 2012, MIT Sloan Management Review, states that "Companies with social and environmental policies significantly outperformed their counterparts over an 18-year period in terms of both stock market and accounting criteria, such as return on assets and return on equity."[7] Plus, it's just simply the right thing to do.

Incorporating sustainability policies and green initiatives into your field service organization eliminates waste and may have profitable benefits. For example, you may be able to recycle or refurbish used parts that can then be resold or used for warranty repairs. In other cases, you may be able to charge for services such as disposal of oil products or the recycling of unusable electronics. You may also be able to reuse parts instead of disposing of them.

You need to stay abreast of changes to regulations or new legislation which affect your manufacturing and field service operations. You must adhere to standards such as Restriction of Hazardous Substances Directive or RoHS. This directive was adopted in February 2003 by the European Union. It restricts use of six hazardous materials in manufacturing various types of elec-

---

7. R.G. Eccles, I. Ioannou and G. Serafeim, *The Impact of a Corporate Culture of Sustainability on Corporate Behavior and Performance*, Working Paper 17950. National Bureau of Economic Research Working Paper Series. Cambridge, MA. March 2012.

tronic and electrical equipment. It is closely linked with the Waste Electrical and Electronic Equipment Directive (WEEE) 2002/96/EC which sets collection, recycling, and recovery targets for electrical goods and is part of a legislative initiative to solve the problem of toxic e-waste.

RoHS changed manufacturing around the world as the European Union requires RoHS certification for electronics sold within the EU. It restricts the use of the following six substances: lead, mercury, cadmium, hexavalent chromium, polybrominated biphenyls, and polybrominated diphenyls. Not only must manufacturers be compliant with these standards, but servicing equipment in the field with compliant replacement parts and disposing of old or repaired parts are controlled.

Of course, there are many other laws in the Unites States and around the world addressing environmental issues. For example, the Chinese government has addressed their pollution issues through their newest 5-Year Strategic Plan and will be focusing on cleaning up the environment as well as restricting future manufacturing and polluting entities.

You will also want to develop environmental policies in case of disaster. You don't want to be known for bad policy or carelessness with respect to the environment. The ill will that is created when something terrible happens such as Exxon Valdez or BP Louisiana oil spills may never go away. You are better off taking preventative measures than to clean up after the fact.

So how do you get started developing a sustainability policy for field service? We often encourage our clients to start with benchmarking. Arrange for some meetings with field service executives in well-respected nearby companies. These companies need not be competitors or partners because you are not going to be investigating operational processes. Begin by asking well-prepared questions about their approach to sustainability. After three or four of these meetings, you will begin to see patterns emerge, and you will have gathered many new ideas.

You can also research recommendations published by professional organizations such as the American Electronics Association, Automobile Manufacturers Association, and Technology Services Association. You should also check local waste management companies and the local dump. You might be pleasantly surprised by the information and help that are available.

In the end, you need to develop the environmental and sustainability policies right for your own organization and support the needs and requirements of your customers.

18 Build and Maintain Accurate Installed Base Data

As-built or as-installed BOMs and installed base accuracy are essential.

Friday, 11:30 PM: Your service team receives a call from your most important customer, who has a 4-hour response contract. Your field engineer is on-site in 30 minutes, troubleshoots, and orders a part, only to discover it is not stocked at your local depot. Your customer will have to wait 12–24 hours for delivery from your national distribution center.

> **Result:** frustrated engineer, very angry customer, and maybe breach of contract

> **Root cause:** supply chain error? No. Installed base error? Yes. Custom configuration not reflected in your service installed base data

This is a common scenario at companies where custom-configured and custom-built products are the norm. Often, engineering change orders or specific customer requests are not well documented. Products are shipped without an as-shipped bill of material (BOM) or configuration documents, or your service systems are unable to support custom configurations. This becomes a significant problem when your field service engineer (FSE) is charged with fixing deployed customer equipment. The FSE may be surprised by the configuration and may not have the correct parts to repair the equipment or may not be able to properly troubleshoot the custom configuration. The only thing a FSE can do is physically examine the equipment then call back to technical support to sort out the correct configuration and get assistance with troubleshooting.

Companies could mitigate this risk by stocking one of every replacement part locally. But this will cause a significant additional investment (we have seen as much as 30%) in field inventories to support the unknown when there are no as-shipped BOMS.

Companies' ERP systems can capture "as-built" or "as-shipped" BOMs and configuration documents including engineered-to-order schematics if product profiles are set up properly. These systems document what exactly has been shipped and can be used as a guide for field stocking as well as FSE training. ERP systems capture this information either directly or through interfaced systems such as document management and engineering software.

Even with flexible and robust ERP systems, red-lined (manual) engineering changes must be uploaded into the system of record for accurate accounting of what has shipped. This is typically a manual process prone to mistakes and can take time to complete.

How can this still be a problem in our "information age" in spite of very good ERP and other supply chain systems? There are two causes: First, there is nearly always latency in uploading and processing of information. Delays like this in any supply chain information system result in larger inventory investments and lower customer satisfaction. Reducing latency in the supply chain will save you money and improve customer satisfaction and loyalty. Second, your ERP and product management systems may not be set up to deal with custom-configured product support in the field.

Customers contribute to service failures by not documenting and advising of changes they make to equipment. Industries, such as telecommunications and oil & gas, are constantly reconfiguring and relocating their equipment. Unless you have dependable mechanisms and incentives to capture this information and adjust both your field inventory and field engineer training, you will fail. Actively encourage your customers to carefully document any changes they make to your equipment.

These types of configuration and as-installed problems can be acute if you are under a customer contract for fast response times. Without as-installed information, updated frequently for changes made by the customer or your field team, fast response may be impossible.

Accurate, timely installed base information is a foundational building block for superior service. Capturing this information also has long-term ramifications for product development and sales. With accurate installed base information, you are better able to plan enhancements, identify markets for upgrades for your products, and proactively manage end-of-life support.

19 Train Your Teams to Deal with Counterfeits

Your field service people are best to recognize and deal with counterfeit parts.

Counterfeit parts can have significant impact on equipment operations or may cause safety hazards and endanger lives. For example, a counterfeit part installed in military or commercial aircraft may cause malfunctioning of other systems and result in deteriorated performance or even loss of the aircraft. In 2011, the Senate Armed Services Committee held a hearing on counterfeit parts in defense supply chains, including electronic parts used to manufacture weapons and other equipment. Investigators found that counterfeit or suspect electronic parts were installed or delivered to the military for weapons systems, including military aircraft such as Air Force's C-17 and Marine Corps' CH-46 helicopter.

Counterfeiting is not limited to defense goods. Any electronic gadget or equipment, automotive parts, industrial goods, and other products might include some counterfeit parts. Counterfeiters are getting better and better at it. It is so difficult to tell counterfeit from legitimate parts, that industrial buyers are often fooled. Even the price of counterfeits may be equivalent or close to legitimate parts, thus eluding suspicion about parts origins. Counterfeit parts may cause your iPod, laptop, or car brakes to fail early.

The only way to control counterfeiting is to maintain control over your entire worldwide supply chain. This means verifying and monitoring suppliers, distributors, subcontractors, and manufacturers, a daunting task where you will need to work with your sourcing and procurement departments.

China is the largest source of counterfeit items. Trade figures show approximately 80% of bogus items across all industries come from China, where there are few legal restraints to control counterfeiting. Eastern Europe, South America, and the Middle East are also known sources of counterfeits. Using the latest manufacturing and printing technologies, counterfeiters are able to duplicate finishes, stenciling, print boxes, labels, and security codes that mimic those on genuine products. Many fakes are undetectable to average field service personnel.

Develop a process for FSE or FSR to handle situations when counterfeit parts are discovered in the field. It is possible that your customer has knowingly purchased and installed a counterfeit part to save money or because genuine parts were not available when needed. Your customer may or may not know that there are counterfeit parts installed, and your field service person will have to break the news. FSEs will need training for this.

First, the field service person should check part numbers to see if any record of serialization exists. If serial numbers cannot be validated, or bogus part numbers have been stamped on the part, the FSE should notify his manager. The next step is to determine if the warranty on the equipment has been nullified because of this counterfeit part.

The field service person should gently explain to the customer that a counterfeit is suspected or identified, and this may invalidate the warranty and cause equipment to malfunction. Ask your customer if he or she prefers to swap out counterfeits for genuine factory parts (at replacement cost, of course) or leave counterfeits installed and suffer warranty consequences. Replacing parts may have significant cost impact to your customers and provide a real business incentive for buying only genuine parts from you in the future.

Counterfeit parts reported back to field service management should also be reported to procurement, quality, and legal departments. Many industry groups such as the Aerospace Industries Association (AIA) also have a central reporting function that allows member to share information and data on counterfeiters.

You can achieve a "win–win" with customers who have counterfeit parts by educating them on the risks of using them and having a "face-saving" way to replace them with your genuine parts.

20 Field Service Feedback Is Essential for New and Improved Products

Customers demand a steady stream of innovation.

Your field service team should be brutally honest in providing feedback on product performance in the field. You now have critical information on customer experience with your company's products. Don't hold back in providing this information to your product management, engineering, and manufacturing colleagues. If they listen with an open mind, they will learn a lot from field service experiences and can determine a path for product improvement.

Product development and product engineering are typically interested in product specifications and features. They should also be intensely interested in getting feedback from FSRs and FSEs about issues with current products in the field and suggestions for ways to improve. These are actions that attract customers and support new sales.

By all means, avoid the "blame game." Engineering and product development may want to "blame" your FSE's capabilities for product performance and extended repair times, and your FSE team may want to blame engineering for developing unreliable products that are difficult to service. Instead, view this as an opportunity for the whole team to analyze and fix product and service issues that are hurting customer satisfaction.

Engineering may not be designing with service-ability in mind. You should change this by having a comprehensive and cost-justified new product introduction process that mandates serviceability as part of any product rollout review. The design may be beautiful, and full of features, but not practical when it comes to serviceability. This is your opportunity to provide design guidance and justify changes based on profitability as well as customer satisfaction impact. Serviceability cannot be just an afterthought, or else, your products will be too difficult to repair.

There should be a steady stream of information coming from field service to product management. World-class organizations facilitate the gathering and reporting of information by providing formal feedback channels (see Rule 3). Typically, this takes the form of FSEs using software to provide informational feedback including a report of findings and suggestions. Data is gathered from these systems and forms, analyzed, and reported to product management and engineering. In addition, the best companies facilitate regular feedback meetings between the departments to encourage dialogue about product strategies.

If there is a perception that your new improved product may be unstable or unreliable, customers will be reluctant to be the first to invest in it. Consider Microsoft's new releases of software are often buggy and unreliable, so instead of investing in new products, most companies will wait for a while to adopt new Microsoft releases until the product is more stable. New product adoption statistics indicate that early adopters are about 13.5% of the population.[8] The rest of us take a "wait and see" attitude.

So why would a company release a product that is buggy? Typically, this is because engineers are up against tough deadlines to stay ahead of the competition and to attract new customers. Release of "new and improved" products is a relentless quest for companies in some industries such as high tech and automotive. Customers expect innovative and improved products and the first to market products typically achieve high market share. So products that aren't quite perfect may be released early. Your company should determine what strategy will be successful. You can approach the best of both strategies by fielding new designs to just a few customers. Having robust field performance feedback that translates quickly to product changes will improve performance and reliability.

---

8. Everett M. Rogers (*March 6, 1931–October 21, 2004*) was communications scholar, pioneer of diffusion of innovations theory, writer, and teacher.

To Get Where You Are Going, You Need a Road Map

A map will tell you where to start and how to get to your destination.

To get on the road to superior field service, you need a roadmap. A thorough and detailed map is best, but even a high-level map will get you started in the right direction.

First, you must identify where you are. We recommend that you start with a thorough assessment of your "current state" which includes identifying these things:

- Describe a typical day in the life of your service organization including management, training, dispatch, call center, and field personnel.
- What is the organizational structure?
- What service products do you offer?
- What are your profit margins and customer satisfaction ratings?
- What are your operational Key Performance Indicators (KPIs)?
- What underlying systems are used to support field service?
- How is your field service organization aligned with your company's business strategy?

Next develop the "should be" or "to be" state. You should think big here and not limit your vision to incremental change. Look outside your industry for service leaders, and utilize their businesses as models. What could or should service be contributing to your company in terms of achieving market share gains for both product and service, overall profit contribution (service margins should be a minimum of 50%), and customer satisfaction? The "should be" state should include your vision, mission, and business objectives for your field service organization. It is important to get these in writing so that you have a framework and context for developing the organization. Make sure your vision, mission, and objectives are aligned with corporate goals. You don't want to have anything in conflict with the general direction or goals of your company. At this point, you may also want to determine any challenges you see as potential roadblocks to progress.

We often encourage our clients to do the "should be" step by hosting a Vision Workshop (as described in Rule 9). In this workshop, people are free to generate as many new ideas as possible. From these ideas, the vision, mission, and business objectives are determined. You may also brainstorm new ideas regarding products such as quarterly maintenance contracts and scheduled "check-in with the customer" calls. If possible, contact a few customers. Remember to review the plan with sales. Ask for feedback to make sure you are on the right highway.

Next, design a draft organizational chart, and assign roles that support your business objectives. Too many companies make mistakes by trying to organize current people and their skills into a chart. This is the wrong way to organize, and you will end up sub optimizing department performance. Determine roles and responsibilities first, and then assign qualified people. It should become obvious where you have gaps in required skills and where you have people that just don't fit into the new organization. At this step, you should also define the requirements to work with other departments. For example, how does purchasing need to work with you to get the right spares ordered at the right time and delivered to the right place?

Next, prepare a detailed roadmap with a schedule of events and action items for the period of time. We commonly suggest (1) immediate action (within two to three weeks), (2) short-term action (90 days), and (3) long-term action (one to two years). Include your assumptions, your projections for revenue and profitability, the process for the development of products, hiring plan, performance measurements, and information systems needed to support the organization. Include communications plans for customers, your organization, and other internal company organizations.

Review this plan with your Board of Directors or Executive Committee. Ensure they are supportive of your direction, and seek their guidance for changes.

Part III
Supply Chain and Finance

Supply chain and inventory are key enablers for delivering superior field service. Finance is the ultimate arbiter of business success: profit or loss. In this section, we address some approaches to the financial service models, review the risks and plan for supply chain interruptions, address trunk inventory, and take issue with the inventory "sacred cow," namely, inventory turns. We close the section with advice on mergers and the advantages of developing a robust refurbishment capability.

Supply Chain and Finance Rules:

- Rule 22: To Bill or Not to Bill—That Is the Question
- Rule 23: Move Customers to an Annual Maintenance Contract
- Rule 24: Anticipate International Supply Chain Kinks
- Rule 25: Trunk Inventories Are Costly
- Rule 26: Inventory Turns Are Irrelevant
- Rule 27: Plan for Mergers and Acquisitions
- Rule 28: Refurbishments Are Profit Enhancers

22 To Bill or Not to Bill—That Is the Question

What kind of contract applies?

Field service organizations are often faced with a dilemma—to bill or not to bill for time and materials for field repairs. The best approach is to have a service contract, but without one, always generate a bill. Your customer will place little or no value on your service and come to expect this for free if you do not generate a bill. Depending on the circumstances and customer relationship, you may collect for repairs, or you may forgive part or the entire amount or apply it to a future service contract.

When determining if you should collect for services or not, first, investigate your service contract with your customer. What kind of warranty and service contract applies?

Savvy companies provide "thin" warranties, such as 90-day and return-to-factory for replacement or repair of failed products. Thin warranties offer the opportunity to sell enhanced service contracts with advanced replacement of parts and on-site repair. These "premium" offerings minimize customer down time and enhance your bottom line. Joe Pinto, SVP of Services at Cisco, says, "Cisco customers have service contracts for support, except in circumstances of warranty. Using contracts reduces conflict over repair and helps us plan our services organization."

But there are some circumstances where billing is questionable. Suppose, for example, that a junior FSE is sent to repair a complex failure. Because of his inexperience, it takes several visits and many more hours than expected. A senior FSE could have completed the repair on the first visit. What do you do? Charge for all the hours and visits? An estimate or NTE amount should be given up front, and the customer's signature and agreement are obtained before repairs begin. Better yet are service contracts that provide unlimited support for a fixed fee or product usage fee. These types of contracts eliminate the need to haggle over the time it took for the FSE to complete repairs.

If the repair is a result of customer negligence or an accident, you should always bill and collect for repairs. You may want to apply some of the cost of the repair to the purchase of an annual contract to cover future service needs. It is helpful to get a customer sign-off when repair work is complete in the field. "We capture an electronic signature from the customer on our hand-held devices," says Damon Schingeck of Markem-Imaje. "There is no delay in billing and no disputes from the customer."

Deciding how to bill may be dependent on the state of the industry and economic environment. If your competitors are strong and offer good alternatives to your company and your products, you may choose to discount services in the short term, in order to retain market share. If your competitors are not billing for repairs, this information should be considered in your decision. But be very careful; the precedent you establish will stay with your company as you grow. Your industry may also determine the approach to billing. Internet and electronics warranties are generally short, and billing for services begins after 90 days or less. Industrial equipment types such as semiconductor production machinery and industrial machines have longer warranties.

The best way to increase revenues is to sell your customer a service maintenance contract. This can be a very lucrative revenue annuity stream where the FSE makes periodic visits to make adjustments and replace consumables for a fixed or performance-related fee. This kind of service contract is especially important for customers where equipment uptime is critical such as dental offices, hospitals, transportation, and telecom.

Service maintenance contracts can generate both high margin and high customer satisfaction, if properly constructed and executed.

23

Move Customers to an Annual Maintenance Contract

Why hassle with your customers over every maintenance action?

We've all had the experience of buying electronic equipment or appliances where the salesperson tries to sell extended warranties. The salesperson starts by telling you all the benefits of extending the warranty, just in case something goes wrong.

The typical warranty that comes with major electronics and appliances covers parts for one year and labor for 90 days. Yet with the increase in focus on quality, most appliances and electronics perform well for two to three years. So the extended warranties that are offered by retailers for up to two or three years are high-margin profit for the seller. Most people know this and decline to buy based on recommendations from authorities such as CNET, Consumer Report Magazine, and other consumer electronics organizations.

Industrial products buyers may not be so sure about declining a manufacturer's extended warranty or maintenance agreement. They are most likely going to evaluate the alternatives, costs, and benefits. If you can demonstrate the benefits, you can probably sell the extended warranty or maintenance agreement.

Your company can benefit substantially from selling extended warranties and maintenance contracts. You have an opportunity to provide superior field service and to sell an annuity that pays year after year. Here are some reasons why you should sell a maintenance contract to your customers:

- Provides continuity of service and allows you to plan revenues and schedule your workers

- Allows product updates on a consistent basis to customers
- Automatically addresses upgrades, engineering changes, and repair issues
- Keeps your equipment in tip-top shape and reinforces brand quality
- Creates visibility into what the customer will buy next and when
- Increases the value of the overall deal
- Creates a financial annuity that could last for many years
- Creates customer satisfaction leading to customer loyalty

"Service contracts are a 'win-win' for the customer and the supplier," says Dillard Myers, VP at Cisco Systems Inc. "With predictable revenue, we can staff the field, and position inventory that enables us to provide outstanding support to our customers."

Service contracts apply to virtually all industries. One of our clients, a dental supply company, was losing money on its field operations. Our project was to consolidate and shut down half of the field operations. While we did streamline the organization, we also focused on selling maintenance contracts to dentists. The dentists were delighted with quarterly maintenance that kept their equipment working properly. Our client turned an unprofitable operation into a multimillion-dollar-generating service group. The dentists and their patients benefited with continuity of service, our client benefited with revenue, and we were heroes.

So what is the best approach for selling maintenance contracts? We find that the sales force may be somewhat reluctant to introduce a maintenance contract, until the end of the sales process. This is because there is a perception that if the product needs to be repaired, the quality isn't good enough. But in our experience, this perception is wrong. Savvy customers of industrial products understand that equipment breaks and needs to be fixed. Further, if you focus on the regular maintenance component of the extended warranty, customers will see this as a benefit to keep their equipment running at peak performance.

Sometimes, introducing a maintenance contract may lengthen the sales cycle since the buyer may need time to evaluate the costs and benefits. Your salespeople may object to this, too. But in the long run, the total value of the deal will increase and thus the sales commission.

We also recommend that the field service people be included in sales processes. At least one meeting should focus on field service and the outstanding organization you have built.

24

Anticipate International Supply Chain Kinks

You need good analytical and financial skills to model service inventories.

If you are a global organization with an international installed base, you must plan your inventories accordingly. This is also true if you are procuring service parts internationally and managing international field service personnel. Handling international service is far more complicated because of time zones, international employment rules, cultural issues, and managing international inventories.

Your purchasing department may be executing purchase orders based on your plan and requirements. You should know if these parts are coming from international vendors. Where you will stock parts and manage stock levels from international vendors raises new issues with respect to inventory investment, quality, and management. You may need to take extra steps to assure your supply.

Some of the things your purchasing department should be doing prior to placing orders for spares with international vendors include the following:

- Qualify vendors.
  - Validate manufacturing capability (visit vendor site).
  - Obtain test samples.
  - Check references.
  - Determine if vendor has schedule capacity to take on more work.
  - Validate international shipment experience and processes.
  - Identify response and planning horizons.
  - Confirm communications capabilities.

- Set up regular monitoring trips to validate the vendor is still producing high-quality parts and following the proscribed processes.
- Identify at least one other alternate source of supply.

You need to determine your spares stocking strategy based on levels of service. For example, do you need to stock spares in multiple international locations for fast response to customers? Or will you stock parts at one or two central locations per region? Your contracts and customer commitments determine your levels of service.

You should rely on your logistics department to determine the optimal approach. Logistics can help you determine the best cost and locations for inventory, identify the appropriate logistics providers, and put a plan together that best serves your customer. They should also be able to help you with import/export regulations and documentation for shipping to international destinations.

You will need to determine parts stocking levels based on historical usage and trends. Start by collecting data on parts usage worldwide, by region and country. Next is to sort data by volume, cost, etc. You might want to determine usage by other factors relevant to your business such as seasonal items and peak usage times. Segregating parts by cost will allow you to leverage the 80–20 rule (80% of the value is represented by 20% of the items) to drive appropriate stocking levels. Many companies offer software packages that utilize this data to recommend inventory levels in support of your committed service levels and, at the same time, minimize cost.

A side benefit of data collection is identifying problematic parts, high-usage or high-turnover items, and quality issues. This is extremely important information for driving field service and engineering activities in proactively addressing safety and premature failure problems.

In our supply chain consulting experience, we find that inventory management for international field service spares and repairs is one of the most difficult and complex challenges to handle due to the number of variables involved. These variables include the prediction of customer needs, maintaining accurate installed base data, and planning for things like natural disasters, import/export requirements, and delays. You will need good analytical and financial skills to model the various options as well as deep logistics expertise for these activities. You can also make use of software (noted above) and techniques called "network modeling" which will allow you to model different scenarios based on emphasizing timing, price, etc. You can find more information about our recommendations for network modeling software in the Software Solutions Appendix.

25 Trunk Inventories Are Costly

Don't touch my trunk.

In our work with a Silicon Valley maker of telephone conferencing equipment, we found their field service people went to various businesses to repair failed equipment in their company cars. Our job was to help this company evaluate and select field dispatch and inventory management software then help them implement it. The company wanted to optimize the field service process and control field inventories.

During the process of gathering business requirements, we learned a lot about their FSEs and how they operated. When their engineer is in the field, replacing parts and fixing equipment, they like to have replacement inventories with them in their car trunks. This means that they carry common parts and swap them out as needed at the customer site. This is good customer service but questionable inventory practice. Field reps end up carrying new parts and failed parts in their trunks or service vans. Headquarters lose sight of the inventory.

FSEs are very protective of their trunk inventories. Otherwise, the FSE would have to troubleshoot the equipment and wait for delivery of the replacement parts from the nearest depot, significantly extending the service call. While the field service organization respects the need for some "trunk stock," they also want visibility of parts in the field.

To make matters worse, when failed parts are swapped out, the old parts remain in the FSE's trunk, sometimes for months. The company had no way of claiming a warranty refund on parts that have been sourced from a vendor. There is poor visibility to failed parts and failure rates. There is little accountability for quality issues.

Most field service departments will claim that they have a process for getting failed parts returned, but it is rarely effectively enforced. Discipline in controlling field inventory—new and failed—is not the field rep's favorite thing to do.

Remedies

We've seen a few creative ways of controlling this problem including the following:

- Withhold incentive compensation from the FSE until failed inventories are returned.
- Include process discipline in this area as part of the FSE's performance evaluation.
- If field service is outsourced, include returns and other inventory control measures as part of the contract.
- RFID or bar code important and expensive parts so they can be tracked.
- Determine a structured inventory profile that should be maintained by FSEs and can only be replenished when a part has been replaced and documented.
- Audit field inventories at least once per year.
- Develop capability to remotely monitor and diagnose problems with customer equipment. Then you will be able to anticipate the need and preposition the parts in the parts depot.

We worked with a distributor of dental products that had an extensive network of FSEs, service vans, and repair centers. They estimated they were losing about $20 million per year in field service. Field inventory was out of control. Warranty reimbursement for expensive items such as autoclave systems was untraceable. The FSEs replenished their trunk or van inventories at will. There was some indication that FSEs took the untracked spare parts to the swap meets on the weekends to earn a little extra cash!

We focused on putting disciplined processes in place, and centralizing dispatch, that included an audit process and check-in/check-out of additional inventory. Ultimately, we took $17 million out of the process by consolidating repair centers and better managing field inventories. We also developed a quarterly service and maintenance contract that was sold to dentists to keep their equipment in good working order. These actions allowed the company to turn a field service profit within nine months.

26 Inventory Turns Are Irrelevant

Customer response time is key.

Remember the Maytag repairman commercials? He lives in a perfect field service world. Your Maytag repairman has nothing to do because the product never breaks. He hangs out, is bored, and hopes the phone will ring so he can fix something.

In this perfect imaginary field service world, inventory turns are zero. Inventory sits on the shelf and gathers dust. But in the real world, equipment breaks, and customers don't want to wait days or weeks to get service. Consider your last experience at the auto dealer/repair shop. If you had your car repaired the same day, chances are the dealer stocked the parts needed or they were delivered from a nearby depot.

There is significant value for customers in minimizing equipment downtime, and that value is directly proportional to the cost and criticality of the equipment. For example, at one of our client's semiconductor chip manufacturing plant, downtime for just one critical machine can cost the company $30,000/hr in lost revenue. Think of the customer reaction to waiting for 24 hours to receive the $20 infrequently used repair part from a regional distribution center.

Once customers understand the true cost of equipment downtime, they are generally willing to pay for the insurance of locally stocked parts. There are many ways to make inventory payments nearly painless, including vendor-managed inventory.

Field service software such as Astea, Servigistics, SAP, and Oracle use mathematical models of inventory parts and service levels, based on variables such as the following:

* Goals for parts response time (from request to delivery)
* Product installed base locations
* Product installed base configurations
* Part usage history, by product and by location
* Part lead times for procurement and repair
* Warranty delivery goals
* Meantime between failure of parts histories
* Repair volumes

On the other hand, no amount of modeling and investing strategies will make your customers loyal fans of your business. If you are looking for great customer loyalty, what you must do is focus on inventory to support your customer's requirements for response times, not inventory turns.

In the airline industry, if you are part of the ground maintenance crew, you know that a flight delay may result when parts are needed for repair. While airlines stock many parts at airports, unusual or very expensive parts are stored at regional hubs. This means that some repair parts must be shipped from another location when a plane is grounded or the airline must substitute another plane to meet the schedule. The airlines call these emergencies "AOG" or aircraft on ground. Now, consider customers upstairs in the departure lounge. They have places to go, people to meet, and things to do. And they expect minimum flight delay due to maintenance. They don't care about inventory efficiency. Paying customers want the repairs done fast so they can continue on their way. If they have to wait, they will choose another airline with better on-time performance.

Remember this airline example when you are dealing with a customer who must wait for your repairs. Optimizing inventory by minimizing in-vestment and maintenance costs may appear to be the right business financial decision, but it rarely builds customer loyalty. Your company financial managers may argue for less investment in inventories, but you need to help them understand that this may significantly impact customer service and loyalty. If it's easy for your customer to switch to a competitor (such as airlines), they will.

So there is an important trade-off between inventory levels and locations vs. customer service and response times. Which is more important to your company?

27 Plan for Mergers and Acquisitions

Are corporate marriages made in heaven or hell?

Mergers and acquisitions are often the result of companies trying to expand product lines, balance market risk, or move in a new strategic direction. Many fail. The point of view during the M&A process is typically a financial or market-driven perspective, not a field service perspective. It would be rare for a company to consider field service as an important component to M&A deals, yet it is very important because field service is the organization closest to the customer. How well field service performs will be reflected in customer satisfaction and loyalty, important things to consider during an acquisition or merger. Field service will also provide clues about service business margins, installed base, inventory assets, and customer response times, which are key performance measures when acquiring businesses.

If your company is acquiring another, volunteer early to be part of the due diligence or integration team. Your company's field service approach, philosophy, processes, and compensation may be quite different from the target company. These things will have to be rationalized during integration. Most M&As count on efficiency savings from the consolidation of core processes like field service and logistics. This requires significant business process redesign and change management for integration. Typically, you would convert the acquired company's processes and IT systems to yours as quickly as possible, unless they have something that is significantly better. Although painful at the outset, early conversion results in significant benefits in performance consistency and earlier realized savings.

Because field service is the organization that most often touches the customer, it is most likely where customers will ask about how the merger or acquisition will affect them. Your field service team should be briefed on how to officially answer. Script the Q&A so that your field service people can answer customers efficiently and accurately.

Meanwhile, you will have much work to integrate an acquisition into your field service organization. You should do the following:

- Establish an integration team, led by your best manager; include yours and their most knowledgeable and best players.
- Identify "current state" of field service at the acquisition by
  - interviewing key field service personnel,
  - sharing your current processes with their FS leadership,
  - encouraging all parties to ask questions and get familiar with how each other's processes work,
  - diagraming their current processes, and
  - documenting KPIs already in place.
- Document best practices that you might want to adopt across both organizations.
- Document IT systems used to support field service.
- Evaluate the workforce (Are FS people representatives? technicians? engineers?).
  - How are they measured?
  - How are they compensated?
- Determine what "future state" processes and KPIs
  - focus on simplification, taking time, and complexity out of processes,
  - get agreement on the right KPIs to measure processes,
  - determine measurement intervals, and
  - set KPI goals and targets.
- Develop a roadmap for implementation.
- Determine who will audit and what and when new processes will be audited.
- Communicate plans throughout both organizations.

Setting and communicating clear policies and standards will help to ease the transition for everyone. Keeping field service in a fog of ambiguity will cause frustration and poor customer service. Instead, set very clear policies and standards, and reinforce messaging around these topics regularly and often.

Change management and organizational readiness assessments are worthy investments whether your company does CM internally or hires outside consultants.

The key to M&A success is helping employees to manage change and minimize disruption in the workplace so they return to working normally very quickly.

28 Refurbishments Are Profit Enhancers

Things aren't always what they appear to be.

I was surprised recently when I took my broken cell phone back to the Verizon store and was offered a refurbished phone as a replacement. It was still within the warranty period, but what I hadn't known was that warranty guaranteed refurbished and "like new" parts. Later, I also found out that people at the service desk were not Verizon employees but were contracted by a local contract manufacturer to provide this service (as discussed in Rule 16). Things aren't always what they appear.

Refurbished parts are components that have been used and then repaired or remade to be sold for warranty and non-warranty repairs. In electronics, refurbished parts are commonly used to repair computers, routers, printers, keyboards, etc. Take Dell computers, for example. If a part such as a keyboard on your Dell laptop fails, Dell will exchange your keyboard for a refurbished one via two-day delivery. You are expected to disassemble and reassemble your own laptop to install the new keyboard, following the written instructions that come inside the box.

In the computer world, refurbished equipment was probably not defective in any way; it may just have been returned. When hardware is refurbished, the components are examined, and non-working parts are replaced.

Refurbished parts for use in repairs can create additional margin for your field service business. Using these parts has another benefit: pricing other repair vendors out of the market if you only allow other repair companies to buy and use new parts. Meanwhile, you use refurbished parts with significant markup, sometimes as high as 75% or more. If you are doing refurbishment overseas in a low-cost labor market, the financials may be even better.

Remanufactured parts are frequently used in the automotive industry and industrial machinery. Remanufacturing includes disassembly and recovery at the part module level and possibly at component levels and requires the repair or replacement of worn-out or obsolete components. Parts that are consumed or worn through usage are replaced. A remanufactured auto part or an industrial machine is expected to meet the same customer expectations as new machines, and they are usually warrantied that way. There are even organizations dedicated to remanufacturing and refurbishment such as the Automotive Parts Remanufacturers Association (www.apra.org).

Another reason customers may want to buy refurbished parts is to maintain a standard across the entire organization. If refurbished products or parts are used, all equipment can be standardized for repair, upgrade, and version control, even if the model or software level is aging. This strategy will reduce the total cost of ownership (TCO). There may be additional financial strategies for choosing refurbished hardware such as a corporate plan to maintain desktop computers for three years before upgrading to newer ones, in order to fully depreciate the assets.

Refurbishment is a win–win for both your company and for your customers. Your field service organization will benefit from the great margins you make on using refurbished parts in service contracts and warranties. Your customers will benefit from less-expensive parts and lower warranty costs while making use of good-as-new parts. To take advantage of both service and warranty programs using refurbished parts, be sure that this is specified in your contract with your customer and they clearly understand that refurbished parts are going to be used.

You should also work closely with your legal department to make sure warranty contract language is clear and parts sold "same as new" carefully follow legal definitions.

Managing your entire service supply chain to maximize the use of refurbished parts will increase customer satisfaction, protect your intellectual property, and enhance your profitability.

Part IV
People

It's cliché but so true—great people are the corner-stone of any business. In field service, the field teams are the difference between failure and success. In this section, we address acquiring and retaining the best talent, the importance of training the team (and the potential for a profitable training business), determining field service technician cat-egories, and planning and staffing for successful international field service operations. Follow these rules, and plan on delivering superior field service with an "A" team.

People Rules:

- Rule 29: Talent Acquisition and Retention Can Be Challenging
- Rule 30: Design Your Service Organization Then Add the Right People
- Rule 31: Pay Attention to Your International Organization or Pay the Price
- Rule 32: Get the Right Fit for Your Business—FSEs vs. FSRs vs. FSTs
- Rule 33: Deploy International Field Service Staff Selectively and with Care
- Rule 34: Field Service Is Your Second-Best Sales Force
- Rule 35: Train, Train, Train
- Rule 36: Training Can Be Profitable

Talent Acquisition and Retention Can Be Challenging

The nature of who you need in the field is changing.

In the 1980s and 1990s, we used to hire great mechanics, electricians, plumbers, and other workmen for field service operations because this was the talent required for the job. But with the addition of sophisticated software and electronic components, the nature of who you need in the field is changing. Attracting and retaining top talent, relevant for today's environment and today's equipment, is a challenge now faced by most organizations.

In the field today, more engineering skills are needed to diagnose issues and understand the complexity of software and hardware interaction. In the electronics industry, for example, companies now hire engineers with college degrees for their field staff. Maintaining a high-performance college-educated field service staff takes more money for salaries and the ability to provide challenging work. Degreed and skilled engineers need to be challenged, supported, and encouraged.

In addition, there is a remarkable rise in the crossover of engineers to different departments and collaboration between product management, product development, and field service. The product performance information that engineers discover in the field must be fed back into product management and product development for continuous product improvements. World-class organizations are beginning to blur the lines between these functions and assign people to move between them. This is an attractive crossover training proposition to most engineers because it enables them to broaden their experience and work on more interesting projects.

The best companies also seek out and hire "A" players and won't settle for less. Recruiters now work with LinkedIn and other online tools to search far and wide for the best talent. As Jim Miller, VP of Google Operations, stated, "I hire only 'A' players because I want the best to enable us to innovate. 'A' players also attract other 'A' players." As your organization develops a reputation for being a good place to work because of challenging work, good compensation, and regular recognition, you will attract those "A" players.

Dr. Jan Ferri-Reed, coauthor of *Keeping the Millennials: Why Companies Are Losing Billions In Turnover To This Generation And What To Do About It*, offers sage advice and smart strategies for recruiting talented new workers.[9] She recommends the following:

- Partner with experts, consultants, recruitment agencies, and talent acquisition service providers.
- Create employee referral programs.
- Optimize internal mobility.
- Effectively promote and manage graduate programs.
- Recruit globally.
- Seek an outsourced provider when you need to build recruitment capability quickly.

Once you have the best talent on staff, you must make sure you are paying attention to employees' needs and motivations. The best managers create team spirit, provide challenging and interesting work, and liberally acknowledge good performance.

"Pay attention to employees," says Joe Pinto of Cisco. "Acknowledge their work publicly and frequently. We recognize good performance daily. I personally call employees who are doing a good job, to congratulate and thank them every week. I want them to know that we notice their great work and appreciate them."

Final note: As the Baby Boomers retire and Generation Y or Millenial Workers join your company, you need to rethink your approach to managing employees. Gen Y'ers and Millenials are highly sought after for their technological savvy, energetic work ethic and global orientation. These qualities need to be nurtured and developed. Many companies find that these new workers don't always share the same values as older workers, and traditional management methods don't work. This can cause conflict and may result in high turnover for young engineers. Pay attention to and manage the differences in order to retain the best talent.

---

9. *Keeping The Millennials: Why Companies Are Losing Billions in Turnover to This Generation and What to Do About It.* Joanne Sujansky and Jan Ferri-Reed. Wiley, 2009.

30 Design Your Service Organization Then Add the Right People

It's a mistake to shoehorn each person into the org chart.

When trying to achieve something different with their field service organization, managers often take the current staff and shoehorn each person into a new organizational chart. This is a common mistake we see over and over in our consulting work.

To design an effective new organization, first, draw an organizational chart that includes the roles and responsibilities you think will be required to support your primary goals (see Rule 21). Do not assign any names to positions at this stage. Instead, determine the skills and attitudes required for each role. Next, apply standard organizational design principles, which you can find written about extensively in books and online articles. They include the following:

- There is no one single "best" way to organize—different systems or designs can lead to the same end—so try different models.
- New design must align with your company's annual goals and enable your organization to execute its defined strategies. These strategies should always place customers front and center.
- New design should direct attention to a particular set of prioritized issues or concerns—design for what you want to achieve.
- New design should signal where field service will focus its efforts and resources, facilitate the accomplishment of work, and motivate job performance.
- New work should be fundamentally different. People should not be working harder at the same tasks.
- Performance should be measured so that continuous progress can be made.

- Various parts of the organization should fit together and must be "plug compatible" (i.e., field service with sales, purchasing, operations, etc).
- Management must guard against going back to the status quo.

Once you have drafted the new org chart and defined roles, the next step is to assign staff to these defined roles. At this point, it should be clear which people have the skills to support the new organization and which people do not fit. Those that do not fit will either need to be re-trained, coached carefully, or assigned elsewhere in the organization. In some cases, it may be appropriate to ask these people to leave your company. Keep in mind, that to change the organization, it typically means you must change the people—sometimes all of them. Although a tough reorganization may be a difficult situation, it may be necessary to achieve different results and new goals.

If you have a global organization, you will have to make some additional decisions about reporting structures. Will you have everyone report into a corporate structure or report into a division, country, or regional manager? Some companies chose the latter for direct reporting to a country manager and also maintain a dotted-line structure to corporate field service for policy and procedures. These kinds of organizations typically hold regular global field service meetings to update the global staff. Technologies like telepresence enable you to organize virtual meetings and conserve travel dollars. It's important to do at least yearly "face-to-face" meetings with the global staff to build teamwork and facilitate inter-team relationships. Keep in mind that employment laws are different in each country. To comply with these laws, ask your HR department for assistance.

The book *Good to Great* by Jim Collins recommends that "you have to get the right people on the bus and the wrong people off the bus." The right people in the right roles will make things happen. The wrong people will slow you down or, worse yet, work against you.

The organization chart doesn't have to be perfect, but having clear lines of authority and well-defined roles and responsibilities tied to your organizational goals will go a long way in enabling your team to work efficiently.

Pay Attention to Your International Organization or Pay the Price

Design your global organization to support your goals.

Rather than sending your local people abroad, you may want to consider a global organization staffed with people in various countries or regions. To design such organization, first, identify what goals you are trying to achieve. Here are some to consider:

- Cost savings due to reduced travel expense
- Cost savings due to different labor rates in different countries
- Improved customer response time
- Improved customer satisfaction
- Improved customer relations through the use of local service people
- Support for the growth and strategy of your company as you expand worldwide

Match the goals you identify with the goals of your organization. Are all goals in alignment? They should be. If they aren't, align them before you go further.

Next, gather data that will support your organizational development. Begin by analyzing where your customers are by country and region. Determine the expected revenues and forecasted repairs from field service operations in each country and region. Research the availability of potential staff in each area plus labor rates, employment practices, and typical benefits.

Use the same process steps we provided in Rule 30. With these goals and data in mind, design a few alternative organizational charts that will support you. Focus on the roles that belong on the chart, but don't put any names in any boxes just yet. Experiment with different models for organizing, and get input from your peers and your boss. Which of the alternative org charts will help you to achieve your goals? Remember multiple time zones, communication challenges, and cultural differences will complicate matters.

Once your draft organization is designed and is in alignment with your overall company organization, then begin to assign names to the various roles. Don't get trapped into assigning people to the same old role just because they have done this job for many years. Instead, focus on how you can assign people to support the organizational goals. If you are setting up new organizations in new regions, try to detail the roles you have in mind. This will help your HR staff and recruiters to understand what kinds of candidates you are looking for.

Survey your current staff and ask for international volunteers. Give your best workers a chance to work where they want and to step into new roles if they prefer (see Rule 29). Your strategy may benefit by using a mix of local hires along with some corporate or expatriate assignments to give the organization a global perspective. Engage your HR department to help with staffing.

Next, determine the Key Performance Indicators (KPIs) that you will use to drive the organization and measure the people. We recommend the following:

- Revenue achieved to target
- Expense to revenue ratio achieved
- Utilization rates for field service people
- First-time fix rate
- Call center response time
- Contract renewal rate

Whatever KPIs you chose, be sure they are just a few important ones, are meaningful to your business, and will help you achieve your goals. Dillard Myers (VP of Global Services at Cisco Systems) says, "You can't get what you don't measure." He uses KPIs to set and evaluate each team member's performance objectives.

Review your organization on a regular basis or at least once per year. Make changes where necessary to realign your goals or when the business environment has changed enough that you need to rethink your approach. Don't allow your organization to stagnate. Remember, field service is good business, and your competitors are always on your tail.

32 Get the Right Fit for Your Business—FSEs vs. FSRs vs. FSTs

A rose by any other name would smell as sweet (Shakespeare).

Throughout this book, we have referred to field service staff as FSEs or FSRs. In practice, field service professionals have various titles including Field Service Engineers, Field Service Representatives, and Field Service Technicians.

Here is an explanation of titles, roles, and responsibilities. Match the right roles and responsibilities for your organization to accomplish your goals.

Field Service Representatives: FSRs are generally the fixers of common problems in the field. They are mechanics, electricians, and plumbers and work on basic products. They usually have a high school education and some technical school. They diagnose common problems and fix them in the field. For more complex problems, they rely on technical support from escalation engineers in the call center.

Base pay range: $50K–$100K plus overtime (typically 10–20%)

Field Service Technicians: FSTs are more technical than FSRs and work on more complex products and problems. They use advanced diagnostic tools such as computers, gauges, and meters to address problems. They can troubleshoot and fix most problems in the field, including software problems. They generally have completed coursework from a technical institution or community college. For more technical or engineering problems, they rely on senior technical support from escalation engineers in the call center to diagnose complicated situations.

Base pay range: $50k– $100K plus overtime (typically 10–25%)

Field Service Engineers: FSEs are trained as engineers and are able to diagnose and fix technical problems in the field on products. Most have college degrees. They may be sent in after the FSR or FST to evaluate and fix more technical and complicated problems. FSEs are the primary field staff used for highly sophisticated, complex products. For the most challenging engineering problems, they call on senior escalation or design engineers at corporate for help.

Base pay range: $85k–$150K plus overtime (typically 15–20%). Some are salaried and exempt from overtime.

Internal support people: There may be several categories of internal support people including call center technical support people, dispatchers, and administrative personnel. These people are also vital to the success of the overall field service organization.

Pick the titles that best fit with your organization. For example, at Jim's former company, Cymer Inc., the field personnel are all FSEs because the equipment that is serviced in the field is highly technical and requires engineering skills to diagnose and fix problems. For other companies such as your local cable company, the first level of field personnel may be FSRs or FSTs, who can install new equipment and swap out parts. For more complicated problems or an escalated problem, the cable company may send a more senior FST or an engineer.

In addition to these titles, there may be some gradation within each classification such as senior FSE or levels 1, 2, 3, etc. These gradations change the compensation levels based on education or experience and allow for a career path. Human resources departments can assist with comparative salary surveys to make sure you are paying competitive rates for your area and for similar job classifications by industry. These surveys will help guide you in developing salary ranges that will attract and retain the best field service personnel.

"If you want the best people, you have to pay them well and respect them," says Michel Yasso of MSR Consulting Group. This includes compensation and titles, as well as how these important customer-facing people are treated.

International Salaries

Salaries can be drastically different from region to region. In China, for example, salaries for field service people are 50–60% less than in the USA or Western Europe. Be sure to check with your HR department to find the current and most appropriate salary level for your company.

33 Deploy International Field Service Staff Selectively and with Care

International field service is complicated.

When servicing your products outside the US, you have a decision to make: hire and train local talent or deploy US field staff. If you expect to have a large installed base of product outside the USA, hiring and training local staff is cost-effective and generates high customer satisfaction. If your installed base is small or if you are at the early stages of international expansion, then you will most likely dispatch field service staff from the USA.

When dealing with international customers and dispatching field staff from the US, a few basic principles apply such as sensitivity to cultural issues, dealing with local labor and environmental regulations, and dealing with counterfeit parts. These complicating factors require the field service staff you deploy to be specifically trained and to be better than the average performers. They also must have a high tolerance for travel and patience in dealing in foreign environments. Of course, there are many things to consider when deploying a FSE to a foreign location. Some of these include:

- Passports, visas, and other documentary requirements for the destination country
- Vaccinations and other healthcare requirements and recommendations
- Emergency information for medical and dental care
- Translators, if required
- Special equipment required such as metric tools and importing/customs requirements
- Lodging and transport to and from customer sites, especially if it is in a remote location

- Length of time the FSE will be away from home. Do you need to provide support for families when an FSE is deployed for long periods?

Be attentive to the needs of people in the field. Weekly conferences with field service management are key to ensure progress and address issues. If field service staff will be deployed for an extended period (for equipment commissioning or extensive repairs), plan for breaks and time off to return home.

High Context vs. Low Context and Everything in Between

Customers are either going to be a part of a "high-context culture" or a "low-context culture." In a high-context culture, things are simply understood between parties. As an example, think of your own family, which is a high-context environment. When family members talk about issues or events, you know the context of the family situation and can abbreviate your time to understand. On the other hand, when you chat with a group of strangers about the same events, you have to explain the circumstances because they do not have the same context or framework for understanding.

China and most other Asian cultures are high context, resulting in an expectation that the field service people will simply understand why something is an issue and will know how to react or behave. High-context cultures may not recognize the need to explain the problem situation in detail as they may assume you will simply understand. In these cultures, Western or US-based FSEs should be trained to ask a series of clarifying questions in order to understand the situation.

On the other hand, most Western and European cultures including the US and Canada are more low-context cultures where customers are more likely to explain circumstances and expectations in detail. Fewer assumptions are made, and typically fewer questions need to be asked. Still, even in Western cultures such as Germany, there are contextual expectations where precision and high quality are the norm.

When deploying international field service people, be sure that they are sensitive to the expectations of other cultures so they can successfully carry out their repairs. Provide training, and dispatch people with care. Websites such as World Business Culture (http://www.worldbusinessculture.com/index.html) provide excellent basic insight into doing business in many countries.

34 Field Service Is Your Second-Best Sales Force

Customers don't think of field service people as salespeople.

Day in and day out, your customer is in contact with your call center and your field service personnel. Because of their role and relationships with the customer, FSEs are in the perfect position to upsell services to improve product performance and address customer needs. FSEs arrive at the customer site with credibility. And most importantly, the FSE should know just what the customer needs, to improve performance and keep the equipment in good working condition. FSEs are your second-best sales force, and they can be very effective.

In our experience working in, and consulting to, field service organizations, we have seen revenues from high-margin services double or triple simply by introducing a commission or other incentive program for FSEs. This can be a very effective way of generating additional high-margin revenues and, at the same time, improving customer satisfaction. But be careful, your field team can lose credibility if customers perceive your team is more focused on selling and on their commissions rather than fixing the customer's equipment.

Most FSE sales programs include incentives and training. Spend time teaching FSEs the process of effective selling. Standardized sales courses are available, but the more effective way is to have your own sales staff teach the FSEs. Some companies compensate both the FSE and the salesperson for service sales, thereby incentivizing people to work together.

Arrange to have your salespeople conduct selling workshops or other formalized training for FSEs.

If you develop an FSE program for selling parts and services, you will also need to develop and implement the associated order processing system. This system should allow FSEs to call in orders or to send orders via online system access. This ordering process is most likely different from other order channels and needs to be thoroughly thought out and designed to accommodate the unique environment of field service.

Finally, a compensation system must be developed to provide adequate incentives. Here are some common parameters for compensation:

Title	Average salary/ hourly range	Average overtime	Incentive for selling products and spares	Incentive for selling additional services	Expected increase in revenue
Field Service Engineers	$85k–$150k (or $40–$50/hr)	15–20%	10% of invoice total	15% of invoice total	2x field parts sales, 20–25% increase in services revenue
Field Service Representatives	$25–$50/hr (or $50k–$100k /yr)	10–20%	10% of invoice total	15% of invoice total	2x field parts sales, 20–25% increase in services revenue

Caution: Managers must be vigilant that the incentives don't cause FSRs and FSEs to sell services that do not add value or cannot be performed. If customers do not see the benefits of add-ons, this may also cause customer dissatisfaction.

So who or what is your best sales force? Your products themselves. If they exceed customer expectations for performance, reliability, and value, your products will go a long way in selling themselves. But when service is needed, it's your field service people who will make all the difference in developing loyal customers. And loyal customers keep coming back for more.

35 Train, Train, Train

A marathon is a journey, not a destination.

If you have ever participated in a 5K, 10K or a marathon, you will appreciate what it takes to finish the race. You assess your capability: where you are and where you want to be. You train to achieve a gradual buildup of endurance and speed. You consider nutrition, health issues and injuries, and proper shoes and clothes. You achieve a balance between exercise and rest. Then there is race strategy. You study and evaluate the course. You consider competition, timing, and race pacing. You plan for how to stay motivated and psychologically positive. And in the end, if all goes well, you finish the race and achieve your goal. But really, it's the process not the finish line that's important.

Training field service is like running a marathon. So many of our clients have made the mistake of training the FSEs on how to repair products but ignore the preparation, strategies, and customer relationships. What they get then are FSEs who function but don't sell or please customers. Companies forget about the balance and variables it takes to have truly great performing field service staff.

To begin, you first must assess the current skills of your FSE team. To do this, ask your top-performing field service people to help develop a list of skills they know are important to being successful. Add input from your sales and engineering teams. From this list, determine the sequence of training required for all desired skills. Next, ask each field service person and their supervisor to assess FSE skills against the list you have developed. Determine training gaps. Generate and administer tests to quantitatively assess capability. Ask for input, as appropriate, from customers.

These skill assessments are essential to develop FSE teams. Use them to determine training plans customized for each FSE. You will quickly see where there are gaps in training and knowledge, and you can track the progress against FSE performance over time. It will also give you a tool to determine which FSE to send to each job, especially when you have a particularly difficult or advanced problem to solve in the field.

The skills assessment, just like an athletic assessment, provides the information to develop course outlines, topics and to determine the type of training: classroom, on the job, computer-based learning, webinars, or conference calls. Once you have a basic plan in place, the next step is to develop the course strategy.

Coauthor Jim Reily ran the Boston Marathon in 2013. To support his efforts, he developed a training strategy regarding his pace, water stops, and how to attack the hills and curves. For FSE training, you also need a strategy that includes the course sequencing, the pace, and how to deal with individual requirements. You'll also need to plan for refresher courses, new product training, and for occasional special classes on a safety problem or quality issue.

The Boston Marathon is a crowd pleaser. Thousands of people stand along the sidelines to cheer runners and motivate them to finish. FSEs must also learn how to please your customers, including how to act, dress, and talk in a customer environment. Customers who are very satisfied with FSEs become vocal advocates for your company and typically continue to spend money with you. FSEs can be your best salespeople for upgrades, maintenance contracts, and repeat product buys. You can train them to become even better.

36

Training Can Be Profitable

Most companies will stratify their training into several levels.

Offering training to operate and maintain your equipment can be profitable for you as well as a major benefit for customers. Plus, it's another lucrative revenue stream for the business. Most companies will stratify their training into several levels.

Level 1 training is generally offered to customers to understand basic operations of equipment and address simple maintenance issues. To be competent at the initial level, customers are trained on equipment operations under various production conditions and the simplest steps to maintain equipment in good working condition. This type of training is typically offered as part of the sales contract where a specific number of training credits are included in pricing.

If customers chose to send more people to basic training, they pay extra. Design your basic training so that it is short enough (just a few days) to entice many customers to attend but detailed enough to give maintenance people a good start. Wherever possible, combine classroom training with hands-on experience on equipment. Basic training will help your customers take better care of your equipment and make it safer to operate.

Level 2 training (advanced basics) may be offered to customers with dedicated personnel capable of performing advanced maintenance or outside people who service your products for fees. This more intense training requires higher level of skills. Training is likely to be a few weeks, depending on complexity of products. Training credits that were included in the sales price of the product could be applied for level 2 training. However, if you want to encourage customers to use your service offerings, it's best to price this training at a premium. This training is longer and more intense and typically justifies increased prices.

Level 3 training is typically reserved for your own company service people or channel partners who provide the most sophisticated repairs. Very often, this type of training includes electronic and mechanical repairs as well as software repairs. As a result, it is designed for only the most advanced students. Most companies restrict this training for only the top performers and senior FSEs because it can put the operation of your equipment at risk if technical repairs are not done correctly. This is also the level at which your intellectual property (IP) is at most risk. Your company needs to evaluate the risks and opportunities of opening level 3 training to people outside of your organization and especially outside of your country where patents are not protected as vigorously.

Providing real, up-to-date equipment for training sessions may be an expensive proposition; however, the training will be much more effective with the right equipment. While you may have been selling your products for years, the majority of people taking your training are representing companies that have recently purchased new, unfamiliar equipment. They should be trained on what they bought.

Train-the-trainer is a popular approach for organizations that have limited training budgets. With this approach, your company trains one or two people who are designated "super users" in their own organizations and are expected to train others. You will have to choose superusers very carefully for their technical and people skills. "At Markem-Imaje we use a train-the-trainer approach. Our superusers are trained on new equipment for 2–3 days, then they train the FSEs. This works well for us," says Damon Schingeck.

To avoid having poorly trained FSEs, you can require all service people to pass a certification test. In addition, most companies will charge to certify people, as certification generally involves testing and review by company product and field service experts. These certification charges are above and beyond training fees and become an additional source of revenue.

Part V
Internal
Departments

In this section, we show how to partner with your internal company critics to achieve "win–win" improvements in product and field service and how to best utilize company executives as customer executive sponsors to improve customer collaboration and loyalty. Finally, we call out two special internal groups that merit special attention as their help will help you deliver superior field service.

Internal Departments Rules:

- Rule 37: The Toughest Customers Are Your Internal Friends
- Rule 38: Avoid the Executive Tourist Trap
- Rule 39: Channel Executive Involvement
- Rule 40: Build a Strong and Effective Relationship with Your IT Team
- Rule 41: Dealing with Procurement Is In Your Best Interest
- Rule 42: These Are Our Rules—What Are Yours?

37

The Toughest Customers Are Your Internal Friends

True friends will be honest.

Your internal customers may be your harshest critics and have the highest expectations, but they can also be your best friends. These supporters and detractors can help you provide superior service.

Critical internal functions in support of field service are finance, sales, product development, product management, and manufacturing. Let's start with finance.

Your finance team should provide you with your department financials including profit and loss statements, analysis of deviations from budget, personnel utilization, overtime rates, and general financial analysis of operations. Build a very strong relationship with your financial analysis team so you can jointly address financial performance issues on a regular basis. Weekly reviews are optimal; monthly reviews should be the minimum. Your finance partners can help you design financial Key Performance Indicators (KPIs) and design reports that will help you control your business. They are good at this; let them help you. Most importantly, finance can help you identify how to drive your margins and profitability up and assist in building your internal company story. This is key to getting other internal departments to work with you on selling and supporting your field service business.

Sales is another critical partner in your success. Best-in-class companies have dedicated field service sales teams. These companies outperform rivals in year-over-year service revenue growth (9% vs. 6%) and contract renewal rates (61% vs. 41%).[10] If you don't have a dedicated team, your company's product salespeople should introduce you to customers. This is because of field service's role in improving customer satisfaction and differentiating your company's offerings from those of a competitor. If you cannot demonstrate good reason for introducing field services to customers, salespeople will tend to view you as a burden, responsible for delaying the sales cycle.

Product development and product management may not consider service input. They are driven by time-to-market urgency and can't always devote resources to design products for reliability and service-ability. To win this argument, you need to demonstrate the negative impacts on customer loyalty and company profitability resulting from frequent product failures (reliability) as well as frequent and extended downtime (serviceability). Quantify the impacts in lost sales dollars and margin reduction. Be willing to assign your top FSEs on a rotational basis to the product departments. The benefits to overall product quality and resulting customer satisfaction will be significant.

Manufacturing and service are often critical of each other. Field service personnel are likely to blame manufacturing for delivering poor-quality products. Manufacturing may blame field service for incompetence in repairing products. To resolve this conflict, form a close working rela-tionship with your manufacturing organization. Hold joint operation reviews that focus on joint root cause analysis of product performance issues, process, and training.

Overall, it is important to get aligned with these critical internal depart-ments. Set your profitability and performance goals with your execu-tives, and align with finance. Set your compensation goals for service and then with sales. Align serviceability and supportability goals with product development and product management. Align high-quality manufacturing with pride of workmanship and teamwork with field service. Set and keep Key Performance Indicators and conduct oper-ational reviews that focus on getting to true root cause of product per-formance issues.

Most companies understand that the service organization is important because it correlates with customer satisfaction. This satisfaction leads to a consistent revenue stream and new business for the company. Sustained field service business typically has high margins and low cost of sales. Loyal customers pay their bills on time, willingly contribute new ideas for product development, and, most important, continue to buy your company's products and service offerings. As a bonus, loyal customers help evangelize your products with other potential customers.

---

10. *Service Revenue: The State of the Market* Sumair Dutta & Aly Pinder, Jr. Aberdeen Group. October 2011.

38 Avoid the Executive Tourist Trap

If you don't have a plan and an agenda, it's nothing more than organized tourism.

Executives will want to speak with customers and make customer site visits. We love the idea that they want to help and add value, but if there is no specific agenda or goals for the customer visit, executive involvement is nothing more than organized tourism. To avoid the executive tourist trap, organize a sponsorship program.

Developing an effective executive sponsorship program requires work and time, but the benefits can be significant. An effective executive sponsorship program can:

- improve communications with your customers,
- enable better understanding of strategic direction of customer's business,
- increase visibility into future sales opportunities,
- defuse crises with customers resulting from performance of your product, and
- highlight process or product problems that you don't see.

To organize an executive sponsorship program, start with segregating and prioritizing accounts by revenue, strategic importance, and those that need high attention. Typically, these programs involve the top 10–15% of customers in terms of revenue. Add customers of strategic importance to new markets and those that can help you expand into current industries. Add customers where problems may be brewing or where your competition has been successful. If you know of potential issues with a customer, they should also be added to your list.

A weighting can be assigned to the customers to facilitate the ranking process. Not all customers in the selected group should get the same amount of attention. Some customers are more important than others and may garner more attention at least in the short term. Some may just be included in customer events, while others, ranking higher, may receive special attention and visits from your C-level executives.

Joe Pinto, SVP at Cisco, told us about their Executive Sponsorship Program for Cisco customers in which all Cisco executives are invited to participate. "Each executive is a sponsor for multiple customers, no matter your functional role at Cisco," says Joe. "You develop a relationship with the customer's executives and discuss business, commerce, how Cisco can help, what Cisco can do better. This is a proactive program and not a response to a customer problem." Executive sponsors can help remove roadblocks and cut through company red tape that may be frustrating the account manager and, more important, upsetting your customer.

Each of your identified top-tier customers should have a profile of information used to brief the assigned executive from your company. This document should include the following:

- Overview of the customer's history with your company including revenues for the past few years, quality issues, and billing problems
- Overview of customer's industry—the biggest issues, etc.
- Organizational structure of the customer, including divisions, business units, and the organizational chart of top executives. The account manager assigned to this customer should have this information and should be included in assembling the executive briefing document.
- Key people you deal with including their roles, titles, and contact information. Who are decision-makers? Influencers? Include an assessment of customer relationships with your company. Are they advocates, neutral, critics, or enemies?
- Explanation of strategy for managing this customer, including schedule of executive sponsor visits, sales opportunities, and associated projected revenue
- Communications and action plan that provides a framework for the next 12 months. (In the following rule, we discuss the plan in more detail.)

Executive sponsorship programs, if well executed, will enhance your overall relationship with customers, build customer loyalty, raise the awareness of customer satisfaction to all of your executives.

39 Channel Executive Involvement

A good executive sponsor will payback her efforts tenfold in increased customer loyalty and revenue.

Now that you have evaluated your customer base and determined which customers to be assigned executive sponsors, you need to develop an implementation and communications plan. Your plan should be simple enough so that everyone can use it as a guideline yet detailed enough to clearly define your expectations. Remember, the goal is to build business partnerships with customers that lead to better collaboration and ultimately repeat sales.

- The communication plan and toolkit should include the following:
  - Calendar of events and activities for the next 12 months including when visits and other meetings will be scheduled, activities such as trade shows, and company events when customers will be invited
  - Quarter-by-quarter activities and action items so that executives can coordinate with their own busy schedules and know what action is required at quarterly intervals
  - Suggested e-mail messages for customers, alerting them to things that are happening in your company and updates on new products and services
  - Suggested agendas for face-to-face meetings and suggested schedule of when these should happen (If you have customer visitor facilities at your company, then remind the sponsors to get the facilities booked early.)
  - Trade shows that are mutually attended and plans for activities and meetings during the show
  - Reporting template for executives to document their customer interaction

- We recommend the following minimum executive sponsor annual activities:
  - One face-to-face meeting per quarter
  - Two to three phone calls per quarter to express interest in building business relationships
  - Sponsoring customers at dinners or other activities during industry conferences
  - Facilitating strategic internal account planning with sales, operations, and service and monitoring progress on quarterly sales goals
  - Getting involved with problem solving when sponsored clients have issues

"I try to visit one customer every week," says Michel Yasso, MSR Consulting. "I try to make sure that the discussion is very specific to their business. That means, I have to do my homework about them before I go. Customers love personal attention."

An alternative to visiting customers at their location is to invite them to your own customer briefing center. This center may range from a nice conference room to a multimedia showplace for your company's products and services. Regardless whether your room is an ordinary conference room or an executive briefing multimedia center, you should show the customer that you really care and are interested in hearing what they have to say.

Cisco does this very well. Cisco's customer center is state of the art in terms of technology and capability. Inside the Executive Briefing Center, the facilities allow for multiple presentations and excellent video conferencing. Customers are made to feel welcome and appreciated. "We discuss business, commerce, how Cisco can help, and what Cisco can do better," says Joe Pinto SVP of Cisco Technical Support. "We try to be very proactive and anticipate our customers' service needs. We listen to what they have to say and assign action items to ensure effective follow-up. The worst thing you can do is listen to customers and then not take action on their suggestions."

In addition, all Cisco executives are expected to participate and present at multiple customer briefings at EBC each quarter. Each executive's presentation is graded by customers attending. The grades are shown at quarterly staff meetings hosted by John Chambers (CEO), so you can imagine there is high motivation to present often and well.

Take advantage of your company's executive talent by having them engage directly with customers. Your customers will like the attention, your executives will get "front line" experience with customer issues, and your company will build loyalty.

40

Build a Strong and Effective Relationship with Your IT Team

Your IT team is critical to your success in field service; you need them.

Ok, so IT folks can be a pain: They enforce annoying password rules, they take forever to get projects done, and they restrict your flexibility and creativity. But they are essential for you to be able to consistently deliver superior and profit-able field service as well as grow your business.

There are two key areas where IT can add huge value to your service business: information and scale.

Information: Your company's IT systems contain an enormous amount of data about cus-tomers, products, and field service repairs. Your IT team can help you turn that data into valuable information. You will need to track what equipment is in your installed base via your En-terprise Resource Planning (ERP) and Customer Relationship Management (CRM) systems. These systems track what equipment was initially sent to the customer (as-shipped bill of material). When your FSEs make repairs, swap out parts, upgrade equipment, or make configu-ration changes; the information needs to be captured and recorded in your IT systems.

Why is the installed base product information so important? We talked about installed base in Rule 18. Consider this situation: Suppose you have a product safety issue and need to know the current configuration of products in order to fix problems. Having current configurations will help immediately identify what needs to be done where. Remember Toyota's problems with brakes? Toyota was able to notify buyers that it had on record. Notification to buyers of used cars, or those sold privately, had to come through expensive and less-effective media advertising. Advertising this way also gave Toyota a black eye.

The best systems track field service performance by recording actual procedures performed, parts replaced, and software changes made for each service incident. With IT's help, this data can enable you to spot early trouble with a new product, analyze performance of your field engineers (time to repair and first-time fix), analyze performance of your field inventory of parts, analyze service profitability of various products and customers, and generate potential upsell leads for service and product upgrades.

Use of systems can help with service product differentiation. When you are able to show your customers that you can effectively track usage of parts and maintain current records on configuration and maintenance, this will have a positive effect on selling maintenance contracts. To prepare for potential sales, mine data that already exists in your systems.

Scale: If you are the Maytag repairman, you don't need to think about scale, but if you have dozens of customers or are planning on growing significantly, then you need the ability to scale your service business. Many businesses have huge numbers of service transactions that are unmanageable without robust ERP and CRM systems. For example, Cisco service handles over 5,500 service cases and ships over 1,200 service parts daily, 24/7/365. Handling this volume of business on a worldwide basis with spreadsheets simply won't work.

To scale effectively and perform at high volumes with no impact on customer satisfaction, you need IT help. Teaming with IT, you can plan the size, geographic locations, levels of system (CRM/ERP) availability, and timeframe for your system needs. Having an agreement with IT on levels of service, planning horizons, and processes for expansion is critical. Frequent operation reviews with IT should be mandatory with emphasis on CRM/ERP system availability as the central topic. Develop comprehensive root cause analysis as well as corrective action plans for any availability failures.

For more information on software systems to support field service, see the Appendix.

Rule

41

Dealing with Procurement Is In Your Best Interest

Today, buyers are better educated and systems savvy.

Back in the 1980s, purchasing departments processed paper POs mostly for production items and repeat buys. Field service engineers (FSEs), who needed parts immediately, purchased them from local parts vendors and charged them to their expense accounts. Without visibility into what was being purchased, service expense, warranties, and performance suffered. We were reminded of this recently while visiting the oil fields outside of Bakersfield, CA.

Near Bakersfield is a small town called Taft, where there are many parts suppliers to support oil field operations. Oil pumps frequently break down and need immediate repair parts. FSEs drive into town, pick up parts, and fix whatever needs repairing in the miles and miles of pumps outside of town. When oil production is offline, it is an emergency; formal purchasing procedures are the last thing on FSE's minds. Time is money in this desert town.

But for most of the rest of the world, times have changed. With the implementation of ERP systems in the 1990s, purchasing departments have improved processes and ability to control maverick buying. Professional buyers are better educated and systems savvy. They think strategically about business and can assist in getting the best deals possible. This is good news for field service.

ERP systems improve visibility regarding parts purchased, frequency, and grouping of parts purchased together for volume discounts. Use your ERP systems to generate purchased-part information reports that help you develop inventory and purchasing plans.

When FSEs need to purchase something immediately, provide credit cards that are tied into procurement and your ERP. These are typically called P-cards. You get visibility into what has been bought and can generate useful reports for controlling costs and inventories from the information gathered.

Professional buyers are trained in negotiation techniques and can lead the charge in rationalizing part numbers and getting the best value in negotiations. Be open with buyers, and describe exactly what you need, so they can help you.

On the other hand, when you are selling services to customers, you are likely to encounter professional buyers from your customer's purchasing department. Buyers will be looking for the best deal to create the most value for their company. Bundling services with the price of equipment is probably the best approach. But be aware that your competitors may separate services from equipment to make their deal look better.

Christine Parlett of Siemens says, "We get a spec or RFP from a customer's Procurement Department, typically just for one product. If services are not requested by the customer, then we add this as an option. We build services and maintenance into the overall offer so customers can choose. We separate out the cost of these extras because if we bundle everything, then our products will look more expensive."

Customer's buyers may want to discuss individual line items and try to squeeze deal margins. Reply by demonstrating the overall value of services and maintenance programs. Here are points to make:

- Cost of downtime: get away from detail level price of each part and focus on total cost of downtime.
- Long-term contracts: this approach will resonate with buyers if they can get a discount for a multiyear commitment.
- ROI for services if they buy from you.
- Industry-specific service: Focus on what resonates with them.

Keep in mind that while the professional buyer is your customer, he or she is not the actual user of your services. If you are able to include the operations people or executives in the services conversation, it will be easier to demonstrate value.

42

These Are Our Rules—What Are Yours?

The Wild, Wild West awaits.

These are our stories and rules and the stories of executives who have worked in field service for many years. But there is so much more to learn and try in field service. Try some new ideas, and soon, you will have stories of your own to share. Become the new sheriff in town, and rustle up some of your own new rules.

What we have attempted to do is provide you with some basic guidelines for field service organizations. As you read this book, you will agree with some things and probably disagree with other things we have written. We hope we have given you some starting points and food for thought.

We have tried to explain a little about a lot of topics and given you some pointers from our own consulting, industry, and military experience. We tried to be the cowboys in white hats and provide you with some guidance and checklists so that your field service business will be more successful. We want you to avoid shootouts with the competition and to win those you are compelled to fight.

And even with all this ammunition, you may still be surprised. Some gun-slinging outlaw may be just around the corner and completely change the scenery. We recommend that you prepare for unforeseen battles through planning and always being open to new ideas.

And so, we end with a few key principles:

- Always put the customer first.
- Listen to what your customers want.
- Investigate what the competition is doing.

- Solicit and act on the feedback from your field service people.
- Treat your field service staff well: Remember, they interact with your customer and represent your company every day.
- Simplify processes.
- Prepare for, and practice, disaster response.
- Measure your performance.
- Organize to achieve your goals.
- Challenge traditional business ideas.
- Don't sell what you can't deliver.
- Under-commit and over-deliver.

Follow these rules, and add a few of your own, and you are sure to be successful!

A | Contributors' Biographies

Morris A. Cohen
Professor, the Wharton School, University of Pennsylvania

Morris A. Cohen is the Panasonic Professor of Manufacturing and Logistics in the Operations and Information Management Department, the Wharton School, at the University of Pennsylvania. He is also Co-Director of Wharton's Fishman-Davidson Center for Service and Operations Management and was Chairman and founder of MCA Solutions (now merged with PTC/Servigistics), which was a software company that specialized in optimized strategic and tactical planning systems for service supply chains in industries such as Aerospace &

Defense, Automobile, Semiconductor Equipment, Computers, and Telecommunications.

His research includes service supply chain logistics strategy and modeling with a focus on performance based incentives and advanced decision support tools. Professor Cohen holds a B.A.Sc. in Engineering Sciences from the University of Toronto, and an M.S. and Ph.D. in Operations Research from Northwestern University.

Jim Miller
Vice President, WW Operations, Google

Jim Miller is Vice President of Supply Chain Operations at Google. In this role, he has responsibility for global operations, planning, supply chain and new product introduction for Google's IT infrastructure.

Prior to joining Google in 2010, Jim worked with leading companies in electronics, networking, clean tech and communications technology, manufacturing and consumer services. His expertise in supply chain, both management and consulting, was honed at Amazon.com, Cisco, First Solar, Sanmina-SCI Corporation, IBM Corporation, Intel and Sierra Crest Consulting.

Jim has a Bachelor's degree in Aerospace Engineering from Purdue University, and Master's degrees in Mechanical Engineering and Management from the Massachusetts Institute of Technology.

Jim serves on the advisory boards of a number of West Coast clean tech and supply chain software start-ups and the Leadership Council of the Corporate Eco Forum. He is also on the Industrial Advisory Board of Purdue University's School of Aeronautical and Astronautical Engineering, where he is a recipient of the Outstanding Aerospace Engineer Award.

Dillard Myers
Vice President, Global Service Supply Chain, Cisco Systems

Dillard Myers has more than 30 years of demonstrated global logistics experience with various governmental and corporate organizations. Prior to Cisco, he held the Marine Corps Senior Logistics Colonel's position on the West Coast, providing total support to more than 45,000 Marines and Sailors. He has had documented success in senior leadership positions, providing vision, focus, and development of supply chain strategies for service organizations having inventories exceeding $6.4 billion and annual budgets exceeding $775 million. Currently, Dillard leads Cisco's Global Service Supply Chain organization supporting more than $8 billion in services revenue globally. He has designed, built, and deployed capabilities to support their customers in 128 countries with 1,100 plus distribution depots.

Christine Parlett
Director Marketing, Strategic Business Development, Customer Service, Siemens

Christine Parlett has over 15 years of domestic and international experience in the customer service industry working for Siemens Industry, Inc. Her background includes development of a service organization in Europe to support the growth of Robicon Corporation, prior to its acquisition by Siemens in 2005. She was also responsible for sales and service programs for the Large Drives division located in Pittsburgh, PA with revenues of $70 million. Christine is currently responsible for driving strategy and growth for the Lifecycle Customer Service division. Christine holds a Bachelor's degree in Business Administration from Seton Hill University.

Joe Pinto
Senior Vice President, Technical Services, Cisco Systems Inc.

Joe Pinto is the Senior Vice President of Cisco's Technical Services group. Through a team of more than 4300 employees, Pinto is responsible for directing programs that improve our customers' experience through product and service quality, including technical assistance, onsite and spare part logistics, CCIE certification, and a wealth of web- and community-based technical support resources.

Since joining Cisco in 1991, Pinto has guided the services organization to anticipate and address the changing business needs of Cisco customers and partners. He and his team have created and implemented Cisco Smart Services, enabling Cisco and Cisco partners to help customers predictably manage the health and stability of their networks, reduce costs, mitigate risk and promote innovation.

Smart Services also support Cisco's overall services strategy by bringing Cisco industry knowledge, expertise, and tools to more customers and partners. With Cisco's foundational support capabilities and smart interactions strategy, Pinto's team works to tailor service delivery to the needs of distinct customer segments and regions around the globe. Today the overwhelming majority of Cisco customer and partner technical support issues are solved online, where knowledge transfer and sharing of best practices have resulted in faster issue resolution, and continuous customer and partner feedback improves services, products, and business processes across Cisco.

Under Pinto's leadership, Cisco Services has received numerous industry honors. To date, Cisco has attained the J.D. Power and Associates Certified Technology Services and Support certification six times, a nine time recipient of the Technology Services Industry Association (TSIA) STAR awards, and a nine time winner of the Association of Support Professionals (ASP) "Ten Best Web Support Sites" competition. Both TSIA and ASP have named Cisco to their Halls of Fame.

Pinto holds a Bachelor's Degree in Business from Golden Gate University.

Damon M. Schingeck
North American Technical Service Manager, Markem-Imaje

Damon Schingeck joined Markem-Imaje in October 1991 as a Field Service Manager based in the Michigan area. Over the last 20 years with Markem-Imaje, Damon has held various management positions in various locations within the Technical and Field support areas of the company and today is responsible for the delivery of Field Service, software/hardware solution development and Level II Technical Support teams for the Markem-Imaje North American Region.

Prior to joining Markem-Imaje, Damon was the Field Services Manager for Michigan Shippers Supply, a large marking, coding and packaging distributor in the Midwest where he was instrumental in developing a field and technical support team capable of supporting over 50+ technologies.

Having worked with companies such as Nestle, Starbucks, Conagra and others in custom developed solutions and support, Damon is familiar with the complexities and hurdles of customer service and support and brings a wealth of knowledge with his 25+ years of field and technical management experience as well as software solution development and deployments with Markem-Imaje.

Damon earned his AS degree in Electronics from ITT Technical Institute and currently resides in Kennesaw, Georgia with his wife and two children.

Michel Yasso
Divisional Sales Manager at Hach Company

Mr. Yasso is an accomplished senior executive with an exemplary record of leading international and domestic organizations in general management, sales, marketing, and value-added services. He is a change agent who specializes in start-up, restructuring, and growth management and is recognized for inspiring and maintaining customer loyalty. He is an innovator that creates and articulates a vision then energizes employees at all levels to exceed corporate objectives. He has a track record of identifying market opportunities that result in new sales, increased profitability, and market share and an outstanding customer relationship management and problem solving abilities. Michel lived and worked for nine years in China developing service, software, and engineering organizations throughout the Asia-Pacific region for Rockwell Automation. In 2008, Michel joined AVL North America, the world's largest privately owned and independent company for the development of power train systems as the Director of Customer Services for NA. At AVL, Michel was instrumental in developing new creative services and increase customer satisfaction.

Michel holds a Bachelor degree in Electrical Engineering from the University of Detroit Mercy and resides with his wife in Rochester Hills, Michigan.

B Software Solutions for Field Service

What to Do First

The first question to ask when evaluating software is "What problem are you trying to solve?" This may seem obvious, but until you identify exactly what you want to achieve and in what priority order, it will be difficult to evaluate your software and hardware options. Are you trying to capture information in the field such as bar codes, part numbers, and configurations? Are you trying to invoice in the field? Are you trying to relay technical questions or information? Starting with a list of what you want will lead you to the potential alternatives.

In addition, work with your IT staff and others in management to determine if your field service information should interface with other business systems such an ERP system and/or CRM system. If so, look for software with interfaces already built or capable of being easily built. You will also have to make decisions about which software will be the "system of record" for inventory, configuration, and other important master data. These are systems architecture questions that are very important to your company and are critical to the successful deployment of software in the field.

You may also want to consider hardware solutions for your field service personnel. In today's field environment, most FS people have smart phones, iPads, bar code readers, or some combination of these devices. If you are working in very remote locations, you may need specialized equipment such as satellite phones or other high-powered communications equipment.

As Damon Schingeck of Markem-Imaje told us, in 2006, they deployed software that required the field service people to be connected to the Internet, so the FSEs couldn't get their work done until they were back at home in the evening. Most of them had families and were unwilling to spend their evenings working. This caused inefficiencies and delays in processing information. Today, his teams use iPads.

Think through the connectivity and interface issues as you evaluate software.

ERP Software

Oracle

Oracle has field service support capability, which includes solutions to support mobile devices for people in the field. However, the E-Business Suite supports only the Oracle database (versions 9i and 10g). Oracle's position is that benefits from the Oracle database deliver more value to customers than being "database agnostic."

SAP

SAP has been improving its CRM product across the board. Laptops, desktops, and tablet PCs support the complete range of mobile service functionality. Key mobile service functionality is also available on hand-held/PDA, smartphone, and BlackBerry devices.

CRM Software

Many CRM systems are focused on keeping track of sales prospects and deal closings for the sales force but not on field service needs. Be careful with evaluating these packages.

Salesforce.com

Probably the most popular CRM software is Salesforce.com, even though both Oracle and SAP have CRM modules. Salesforce.com or SFDC is cloudbased and completely focused on interacting with customers through sales and services. In addition to having field service functionality that is pretty good, SFDC also offers a variety of applications available through its AppExchange. This very popular software has been widely adopted by companies around the world for sales force support. If your company already has SFDC, you should definitely evaluate its functionality for use by your field service personnel.

ServiceMax and Astea

There are also more substantial functional applications such as ServiceMax and Astea that totally focus on field service. If you have a large FS organization and substantial needs, these software packages may be right for you. Be sure to have a detailed discussion with your IT staff first, to make sure that these packages are capable of effective interface with your business systems.

Scheduling Software

There are many software packages that can assist you with scheduling and dispatching field service personnel. ServicePro, Dataforma, and FieldOne are some of the better software solutions for this functionality. Salesforce.com also provides this functionality and should be considered. These software packages are excellent when you have lots of repair people to dispatch on a daily basis.

Bar Code Software and Hardware

There are dozens of bar code hardware and software companies capable of printing and reading barcodes. The most important thing, however, is to make sure that your ERP or other business systems are able to take a data feed from the barcode software and use this information in other applications. Access to information throughout your organization is key to managing the equipment and people you have in the field, plus quality and safety issues, configurations, billing records, and other activities. A stand-alone bar code system won't do you much good. While bar codes may seem like a simple idea, remember, the bar code is a visual representation of a part number which is most likely tied to vendors, manufacturing BOMs, configurations, dates, and customers. It's complicated. If deployed properly, bar codes can offer a world of information at your fingertips. If not deployed properly, you won't get much use out of the system.

Business Warehouse Software

A business warehouse or data warehouse or enterprise data warehouse is a database used for reporting and data analysis in a business environment. It is a central repository of data created by integrating information from one or more disparate software systems that are part of your IT architecture. Data warehouses store current as well as historical data and are used for creating reports for analysis and comparison and trending and emerging ideas.

Work with your IT staff to develop reports from your data warehouse. Use reports to improve your field service such as utilization of FSEs, inventory in field locations, and usage of parts. Use of this type of reporting and analysis has become so important to the management of field service that you may want to have a full-time analyst on your staff to support you in dealing with the available data.

C Consulting Audit Checklist

If you decide to include consulting services in your field service organization, you will need to develop some standardized approaches and deliverables, just as you would expect from any professional consulting organization. This might include an audit document and checklist for use by field service consultants for site visits and consultations and a standardized deliverable report template to give your customer. Be sure to make these documents standardized and used for all client deliverables.

Here is a checklist for site visits and customer discussions:

Item	Question	Purpose
Organization	What is the customer's organizational structure? Where do the maintenance people report?	To understand your customer and the decision-makers in the customer organization
Business Requirements	What are their needs in terms of uptime, etc., to support their internal operations?	Clarifying the customer needs will help you design a customized field service offering that exactly fits their needs
Physical Implementation Site	Where will the equipment be installed?	Knowledge of the installed site will help you determine if there are special delivery requirements, special fittings needed, extra personnel for commissioning, etc.
Servicing Personnel	Who are the customer's people that will be servicing equipment? Are they engineers? Maintenance? Other?	To gauge the customer's capabilities and the potential need for training
Service Desired	Does the customer want 24/7/365? Or something less?	Understanding the desired service will help you determine what level to offer
Parts Availability	Does the customer want to pay for parts to be on-hand for rapid turn-around time on repairs?	Helps you to craft a solution which may increase the value of the overall customer contract. Be sure to match investments in inventories with appropriately priced services
Preferred Communications	What is the customer's preferred method of communication? Phone? E-mail? Fax? Web site?	Helps you to tailor an approach to communications for this customer

Item	Question	Purpose
User Group	Is the customer interested in joining a user group?	UGs help build customer loyalty and relationships with your customer
Feedback to Manufacturer	Is the customer willing to provide feedback on products at regular intervals?	Capturing this information will help drive your internal product development

Appendix

D

Field Service Key Performance Indicators

Here are some common KPIs:

- Equipment uptime: most important overall KPI. Definitions vary by customer (i.e., "SEMI e-10" is a standard measure for the semiconductor industry). Very high-uptime requirements (such as telephone companies) will require equipment redundancy or on-site parts and technicians.
- First-time fix: Was equipment fixed correctly the first time?
- Service response time: customers may say they want 7x24 coverage but only want to pay for 5x12 service.
- MTTR (meantime to repair).
- MTBF (meantime between failure).
- SOFR (service order fill rate): Were you able to deliver all parts needed for repair?
- LIFR (line item fill rate): internal measure to determine effectiveness of your inventory planning systems.
- Distribution quality: right parts at the right place
- Customer satisfaction after repair: How satisfied are they with the service?
- Ratio between planned maintenance and corrective maintenance: this ratio should be ~90 to 100.
- Field engineer utilization: amount of time the service person is generating revenue based on 2088 hours/year/person less vacation/training/holidays.
- Cost per repair action by product line and geography.
- Service inventory efficiency such as value of inventory vs. service revenue or value of inventory vs. value of installed base of product supported. We recommend you avoid inventory turns to measure service inventory (see Rule 26).

Appendix

E

Assessing Your Field
Service Current State

We recommend that you start with a thorough assessment of your field service organization's "current state" which includes identifying these things:

Evaluate	Purpose
Describe a typical day in the life of your service organization including management, training, dispatch, call center, and field personnel	This description will help you get clarity around all of the processes and activities within FS. You may be surprised about what activities consume the most FS time and resources
What is the organizational structure? Formal or informal?	You may think the organizational structure is obvious and well known. But in fact, people don't always know the formal reporting structure. You should also capture the informal structure including who are the "go-to" people in the organization
What service products do you offer?	Identify all of the services you offer including maintenance agreements, break/fix, consulting, and training
What are your profit margins and customer satisfaction ratings?	These two things should be tracked at defined intervals and have KPIs clearly identified and measured
What are your operational Key Performance Indicators (KPIs)?	In addition to profit margin and customer satisfaction, what else are you measuring and why?
What underlying systems are used to support field service?	Identify and document all systems that are used in support of FS. Document all reports that are used and their purpose
How is your field service organization aligned with your company's business strategy?	Document how FS supports corporate goals and strategy. Is the FS organization in alignment or is it disconnected?

Next, develop the "should be" or "to be" state. You should think big here and not limit your vision to incremental change. Look outside your industry for service leaders, and utilize their businesses as models. What could or should service be contributing to your company in terms of achieving market share gains for both product and service, overall profit contribution (service margins should be a minimum of 50%), and customer satisfaction? The "should be" state should include your vision, mission, and business objectives for your field service organization. It is important to get these in writing so that you have a framework and context for developing the organization. Make sure your vision, mission, and objectives are aligned with corporate goals. You don't want to have anything in conflict with the general direction or goals of your company. At this point, you may also want to determine any challenges you see as potential roadblocks to progress.

About the Authors

Rosemary Coates is the President of Blue Silk Consulting (**http://bluesilkconsulting.com**), a global supply chain consultancy and the author of *42 Rules for Sourcing and Manufacturing in China*, a Top Seller on Amazon.com. Prior to Blue Silk Consulting, she was a senior director at SAP, the supply chain consulting practice leader at KPMG Peat Marwick and at Answerthink, and a regional manager at Hewlett-Packard.

Ms. Coates is a Licensed United States Customs Broker. She is also a Lifetime Credentialed Instructor for the State of California colleges and universities. She taught management, international business, and importing and exporting for 10 years.

Ms. Coates has consulted with over 80 global and domestic clients, VCs, and private equity firms on supply chain systems and processes. She has considerable international experience and has worked for extended periods in Asia and

Europe. She has extensive knowledge and experience in manufacturing and outsourcing in China.

One of today's most sought-after China supply chain experts, Coates is a frequent speaker at industry conferences and a feature writer for global business publications. Coates is a member of Reuters Insight, a community of experts, and the Gerson Lehrman Group Experts where she consults on supply chain matters. She often testifies as an Expert Witness in supply chain matters.

She is a member of the Board of Directors for the University of San Diego Supply Chain Management Institute.

Coates holds an MBA in Finance and Operations Management from the University of San Diego and a BS in Logistics from Arizona State University.

She lives and works from her offices in Silicon Valley.

Jim Reily is a Principal at R&R LLC, a field service, service logistics, and operations consultancy. Prior to forming R&R, Jim was the Vice President, Worldwide Service Operations for Cymer Inc., leading the global field service, service parts supply chain, training, technical documentation, and technical support teams. Jim joined Cymer Inc. from Cisco Systems Inc., where he was the Vice President, Technical Support, responsible for Cisco's global network of on-site service engineers, service parts depots, as well as the service inventory management, service supply chain contracting, repair, and quality teams.

Reily served in the US Navy for 25 years as a Supply Corps Officer, specializing in aviation logistics, inventory management, financial management, and information technology. He was the Executive Officer of the Fleet and Industrial Supply Center, San Diego, providing logistics support for the Pacific Fleet Naval Forces, and he commanded the Defense Mega Center, San Diego, providing hosted information services in maintenance, logistics, payroll, and administration for all Naval Forces in the western United States, Hawaii, Japan, and Indian Ocean areas. He holds the rank of Captain.

Reily has spoken at numerous service supply chain, field service, and logistics conferences. He was selected as one of the top e-business and e-supply chain executives for his innovative work on virtualizing service supply chain operations.

Reily holds an MA in National Security and Strategic Planning from the Naval War College, where he graduated with distinction. He also holds an MS in Financial Management from the Naval Post Graduate School, an MA in International Relations from Salve Regina University, and a BS in Industrial Engineering from the Ohio State University.

42 Rules Program

A lot of people would like to write a book, but only a few actually do. Finding a publisher, distributing, and marketing the book are challenges that prevent even the most ambitious authors from getting started.

If you want to be a successful author, we'll provide you the tools to help make it happen. Start today by completing a book proposal at our website http://42rules.com/write/.

For more information, email info@superstarpress.com or call 408-257-3000.

Other Happy About Books

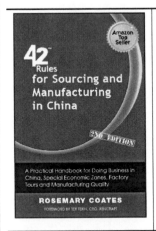

42 Rules for Sourcing and Manufacturing in China

Through over 20 extraordinary executive interviews, Rosemary Coates captured the essence of sourcing and manufacturing in China.

Paperback: $19.95
eBook: $14.95

#CORPORATE CULTURE tweet Book01

Written in the actionable tweet format and demonstrating the value that can be delivered in small packages, #CORPORATE CULTURE tweet Book01 will find a home on every progressive corporate leader's bookshelf.

Paperback: $19.95
eBook: $14.95

42 Rules of Product Management

Learn the Rules of Product Management from Leading Experts Around the World.

Paperback: $19.95
eBook: $14.95

#SCRAPPY GENERAL MANAGEMENT tweet Book01

In the routinely-chaotic world of general management that you live in, you don't have the luxury of reading management books cover to cover, no matter how much they can help you. You need a book that you can flip open and learn something that applies to your world...not next week...not tomorrow...but NOW.

Paperback: $19.95
eBook: $14.95

Purchase these books at Happy About
http://happyabout.com/
or at other online and physical bookstores.

A Message From Super Star Press™

Thank you for your purchase of this 42 Rules Series book. It is available online at:
http://www.happyabout.com/42rules/superiorfieldservice.php
or at other online and physical bookstores. To learn more about contributing to books in the 42 Rules series, check out
http://superstarpress.com.

Please contact us for quantity discounts at
sales@superstarpress.com.

If you want to be informed by email of upcoming books, please email
bookupdate@superstarpress.com.

CPSIA information can be obtained at www.ICGtesting.com
Printed in the USA
BVOW01s1907020414

349571BV00005B/9/P